WHOM NOT TO
Marry

WHOM NOT TO

Marry

TIME-TESTED ADVICE

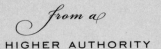

HIGHER AUTHORITY

FATHER PAT CONNOR

HYPERION

New York

Library of Congress Cataloging-in-Publication Data

Connor, Pat, Father.
    Whom not to marry : time-tested advice from a higher authority / Father Pat Connor.
        p.   cm.
    ISBN 978-1-4013-2354-7
    1. Marriage.   2. Mate selection.   3. Interpersonal relations.
I. Title.
    HQ734.C733 2010
    646.7'7—dc22   2009046582

Hyperion books are available for special promotions and premiums. For details contact the HarperCollins Special Markets Department in the New York office at 212-207-7528, fax 212-207-7222, or e-mail spsales@harpercollins.com.

Book design by Shubhani Sarkar

FIRST EDITION

10 9 8 7 6 5 4 3 2 1

THIS LABEL APPLIES TO TEXT STOCK

We try to produce the most beautiful books possible, and we are also extremely concerned about the impact of our manufacturing process on the forests of the world and the environment as a whole. Accordingly, we've made sure that all of the paper we use has been certified as coming from forests that are managed to ensure the protection of the people and wildlife dependent upon them.

To my parents,
Herbert Eli and Patricia O'Brien Connor,
and to my brother, Desmond,
and his wife, Judy Connor—
none of whom needed this book.

Contents

O ver the years, countless women and men from across the country have shared their personal stories with me. Many of them appear in this book. Though I am most grateful for their generosity, I have chosen not to reveal any names or identifying factors. After all, priests are very good at keeping secrets.

Although the advice in this book is intended for those who have not yet married, but are planning to do so, I have sought the example of happily married couples (most of them, anyway) to add their wisdom to mine.

Though this book is addressed primarily to women, men may, like Ruth in the Old Testament picking up the gleanings left behind by the reapers, pick up any insights that may be helpful to them as they mull over whether to choose a particular woman to be their wife.

One of the reasons this book is aimed primarily at women is that my experience is that women usually take the initiative when it comes to talking about relationships, just as it is usually the wife who takes the initiative when it comes to going to a marriage counselor when a marriage begins to unravel. In a word, women are more open than men to discussing "whom not to marry" and more likely to call off a relationship that bodes ill for a marriage. Ideally, I suppose, if a woman finds a relationship becoming problematic, she might persuade her significant other to discuss the contents of this book with her!

*H*ollywood says that if you are deeply in love with someone, your marriage to that person will work. But in my experience, you can be deeply in love with someone to whom you cannot be successfully married.

Romance is a matter of feelings, or emotions, and they're not always the most reliable guides to the truth of a situation. In the courtship phase, the falling-in-love phase, all is bliss: the beloved can do no wrong and you can never have enough of each other's company. You're his Pooh Bear and he's your Love Bug. You forgive those late nights spent with his old college roommate. And when your phone bill goes through the roof you really do believe that "love conquers all."

It doesn't.

A love affair may lead to marriage, but love by itself cannot make a marriage work. When you're in a new relationship, in those first heady days of romance, the man you are dating may very well be a candlelit-dinners-and-long-walks-on-the-beach version of himself. That's not to say he's not being authentic; he's just putting his best self forward to impress you. If you're honest with yourself, you're probably doing the same. (When is the last time you showed up for a date in sweatpants and sneakers?)

A love affair is all about *better* and *best*—that is to say, each date seems better than the last, and of course you're both showing your best selves. Marriage, on the other hand, accepts the reality of *for better or worse*. It's an important distinction to make.

Joseph Campbell may have said it best: "Marriage is not a love affair. A love affair is a totally different thing. A marriage is a commitment . . . a love affair isn't that. That is a relationship of pleasure, and when it gets to be unpleasurable, it's off. But a marriage is a life commitment, and a life commitment means the prime concern of your life. If marriage is not the prime concern, you are not married."

Infatuation trumps judgment, that much I know. Once people have fallen in love, it's hard to get them to think rationally about marriage, to think coolly about the years ahead. I know this sounds rather unromantic, but it's important to think about marriage not just with an open heart, but with open eyes, too. Love may be blind, but marriage is like a trip to the optometrist's office.

The truth is, *I do* does not always lead to *happily ever after.*

The statistics on divorce are depressing. More depressing are the countless unhappy marriages that statistics fail to take into account. But as random as life—and marriage—can seem, there are many things you can do to make sure your life partner is the right one. It all starts with being honest with yourself.

Take my word for it.

For more than half a century, I have officiated at, on average, five weddings a year, or over two hundred weddings. That's a lot of wedding cake.

Each wedding has its own story, of course, and

each couple is unique. Yet I'm constantly amazed that things don't go wrong more often. I remember officiating at a ceremony when I asked the bride, "Do you take this man to be your lawful wedded husband?"

She thought for a while and then said coolly, "No."

That was the end of that.

A couple of years ago in New Jersey, I was at a wedding reception when a full-scale brawl broke out between the members of the groom's family and the members of the bride's. Names were called. Punches were thrown. Tears were shed. All the drama, of course, was lovingly captured on video. Nevertheless, the marriage turned out to be a happy one—though I don't imagine the happy couple looked too often at the video of the reception.

At another wedding, the bridesmaids were sedately proceeding down the aisle toward me, when the maid of honor stepped her foot through her gorgeous gown. The tearing of fabric echoed through the church, closely followed by a colorful word that destroyed for a while the solemnity of the occasion.

Perhaps there has been a colorful word or two directed at me for daring to offer advice on the subject of marriage. You might be thinking, *He's a priest. He's never been married,* and in that you would be correct. But priests, you should know, never hesitate to offer their opinion on matters they seem to know little about. Sure, I completed a master's degree in counseling at Fordham University, and have for decades advised couples on every stage of their relationships. Nevertheless, there will always be a practical gap in my experience of marriage. My involvement is limited, after all. (As Goethe would say, "There's nothing more frightening than the sight of ignorance with spurs on." Put another way, I may put on my boots, but I've never been to the rodeo.)

My own philosophizing about marriage has been directed mainly at those who are beginning to consider it. For over fifty years I have had the privilege of speaking with young women on the subject of whom not to marry. Direct and curious—sometimes blunt!—these women have opened their hearts and minds while bringing me their questions on the subject of marriage and a mate. "What if I don't like my husband's family," they'll ask me. "Is that going to be a problem?" ("It doesn't have to be," I usually respond.) And "Is money really important in a marriage?" ("Yes. Yes. Yes," to that one!) "My friends don't respect my boyfriend because he lets me walk all over him." ("It's good to have a doormat in the home," I tell them. "But not if it's your husband.") And "What if I love him, but know in my heart he's no good?" (My answer to this last question is always to run as fast as you can—in the opposite direction.)

Like any teacher, I have learned as much as I have taught. I am grateful to these young women for trusting me with their most personal dreams and desires.

I hope I have been worthy of their trust.

I hope I will be worthy of yours.

About four years ago one of my best friends contacted me and said, "My daughter Margaret is getting married in New York. Would you preside at the wedding?"

"I'd be honored," I said.

The day arrived, and about ten of us gathered near a pond in Central Park. As the couple prepared to pronounce their vows, a bold New Yorker cried out from the crowd of watchers, "Don't do it! Don't do it!"

When I heard that admonition, I thought of all those spouses-to-be who ever did, or will, hear their own inner voices crying out, before they pronounced their own vows, "Don't do it! Don't do it!"

It is for them that I write this book.

ONE

Before You Say "I Do"

Perhaps it's no surprise that when I invite engaged couples preparing for their wedding day to choose a favorite text for their ceremony, a great many choose those famous words from Paul in his first-century letter to the Corinthians. Anyone who has ever attended a wedding has probably heard those words. I like to list them this way:

- ❧ *Love is patient.*
- ❧ *Love is kind.*
- ❧ *Love is not envious or boastful or arrogant or rude.*

- ❧ *Love is not selfish; it does not insist on its own way.*
- ❧ *Love is not easily irritated, nor is it resentful.*
- ❧ *Love does not rejoice in wrongdoing; it rejoices in the truth.*
- ❧ *Love hopes all things, endures all things. And it never gives up.*

Just as there are seven deadly sins, this beautiful passage offers up seven points of love, each as important as the next in the formation of a happy life and a happy marriage. Over the years, I have thought and prayed over these words, themselves a living text. I have found the test of whether two people really love each other may be found in how they live these words of Paul.

These words are so important that I have used them as the framework around which this book is organized. Understanding what love is—and what it is not—is vital to entering into a happy marriage. I have come to believe that it's easy for someone to say, "I love you." But how easy is it really to *live* that word of "love"?

Paul wrote and spoke in Greek, so he would have known that there are four Greek words for love: *philia,* the love of friends; *eros*, romantic or sexual love; *storge*, sacrificial love, like the love of parents; *agape*, undiscourageable goodwill. All four of these beautiful qualities should be at work in a relationship. Use your good judgment. Know what you want and what in your life is worth loving. Once you can do that, you'll stand a much better chance of living that *happily ever after*.

NEVER MARRY A MAN WHO . . .
THE EXCEPTION AND THE RULE

Before I begin to speak specifically about the kind of man whom my inclination is that you should avoid, I should explain. I used to talk categorically about the kind of man *you should never marry*—but I ran into so many exceptions that I thought I had better modify the force of my advice and say something like this: "Usually it's not a good idea to marry a man who . . ."

- *makes you feel bad about yourself.*
- *cannot say I love you.*
- *refuses to accept responsibility for his actions.*
- *doesn't know how to hold down a job.*

⊰   *has no friends.*
⊰   *doesn't know how to apologize.*
⊰   *is tied to his mother's apron strings.*
⊰   *NEVER marry a man who is cruel to you—*
    physically or emotionally. (On this one there
    is no exception.)

Like any list, this one is just a jumping-off point—a place for discussion and debate. No doubt you'll have your own. No doubt it will be much longer than mine.

A year or so ago, *New York Times* columnist Maureen Dowd wrote about my work in an article entitled "The Ideal Husband." My "mostly common sense advice about how to dodge mates who would maul your happiness" inspired some readers to take immediate action. A friend reported that *her* best friend had broken off her relationship with a man after what she learned from the *New York Times* piece about whom not to marry. In this case it was: "Don't marry a man who is tied to his mother's apron strings."

Letters to the editor flooded in. My favorite came from a woman, twice married and divorced, whose advice—clearly gleaned from wedded life—drew amazing parallels with that of yours truly.

She wrote:

- *Never marry a man who yells at you in front of his friends.*
- *Never marry a man who is more affectionate in public than in private.*
- *Never marry a man who notices all of your faults but never notices any of his own.*
- *Never marry a man whose first wife had to sue him for child support.*
- *Never marry a man who corrects you in public.*
- *Never marry a man who sends birthday cards to his ex-girlfriends.*
- *Never marry a man who doesn't treat his dog nicely.*
- *Never marry a man who is rude to waiters.*
- *Never marry a man whom your mother doesn't like.*
- *Never marry a man whom your children don't like.*

I guess I've been on the right track for fifty years.

TWO

....

Love Is Patient

ABOVE ALL THINGS, PATIENCE

On February 2, 1983, a fire broke out in the residence I lived in with several other priests. By the next
morning, we had lost everything.

In a great outpouring of love and hospitality,
people from the surrounding parishes invited us into
their homes while our residence was being rebuilt.
What a precious virtue the gift of hospitality is!

I took shelter with a very kind family. For three
months, I lived in their basement in the company
of a neurotic dog and a hamster. There were also
four young children in the home who were between
the ages of four and twelve. Having been a priest
all my life, I'd always enjoyed the leisure of a selfish

bachelor's existence. I wasn't used to this sort of family chaos and rubbing of shoulders. It drove me crazy.

I couldn't take it. I couldn't take the daylong cacophony of scurrying and barking that harmonized with the ever-present chorus.

"Mom, where are my ballet shoes?"

"Honey, did you see my keys?"

"David, leave the dog alone."

Grateful or not, I knew that if I didn't get out, I might kill somebody. (Imagine the headlines.) So I packed my bags. But before I left, I had to ask one question.

"Maggie," I asked the mother, "how do you do this? How do you remain so patient in the face of all the demands constantly being made of you?"

"Come on, Pat," she said. "We're Catholics here."

"So?" I said.

"Well, we believe in Original Sin."

"So?" I said. I can be a bit thick at times.

She replied, "So every human being is basically flawed, right?"

I couldn't argue.

"Well," she continued, "think about it. If we're all flawed, then isn't it foolish to expect rational behavior from another human being? I mean, *consistently* rational behavior. Once you begin expecting that, well . . . you're in big trouble."

I needed more. "And practically this means?"

She grinned at me. "I allow my husband two moments of insanity per day," she said. "I allow each of my children three moments of insanity per day. And I've been allowing *you* four."

I was chastised.

It seems amidst the chaos I'd forgotten one of the most basic principles of love: patience. Here was a woman who took an unassailable piece of wisdom— the imperfect nature of humanity—and used it to help her to be patient with the goings-on in her household, and with me.

After thanking her for her generosity those last few months, I left and went to live with two priests, neither of whom was speaking to the other. Now, *that* I could handle!

LIVE WITH PATIENCE, LOVE WITH PATIENCE

It is not enough to simply say, "Love is patient." You have to give the words some foundation.

So what exactly *is* patience?

Patience is that valuable quality which allows us to wait for what we want, to understand that sometimes we have to look beyond the present moment to realize the satisfaction of true fulfillment. More than that, however, patience is the ability to wait without complaint for what we desire—and what we know in our heart we deserve.

Patience gives us the strength to face what is in front of us, while waiting for what may lie beyond us. It's about endurance, staying power, tolerance, and persistence—all good things to cultivate.

You can tell a lot about a person by the way he handles these three things: a rainy day, lost luggage, and tangled Christmas tree lights.

—MAYA ANGELOU

No marriage is ever pure ease and joy. It really is a "for better or worse" arrangement. So how does patience fit in?

Well, for one thing, patience admits the uncomfortable truth that we are, all of us, imperfect. Patience recognizes that often, not only is there a space between what we want and what we get, but between who we are and who we want to be. That means that sometimes we've got to cut each other some slack. Don't demand perfection, because you won't get it. If you can see that your partner is well intentioned, that he respects you and your relationship, then focus on that.

Marriage is a big picture endeavor, and while it matters—greatly—what we do on a daily basis, it's important not to get tripped up by the little things that may go wrong. Be patient, and know that patience leaves room for error. It understands that just as the rose won't sprout overnight from the seed, your husband isn't likely to put the toilet seat down the first time you ask him.

TERMS OF ENGAGEMENT

If patience is a useful trait during marriage, it can be even more valuable before the marriage takes place. There's no harm in waiting a while between the engagement and the marriage ceremony. In fact, a decent waiting period can be a very good thing because it will give you and your fiancé an opportunity to evaluate your relationship.

Chances are, when you look at your boyfriend, you probably think about how he measures up as a *boyfriend*. But have you given any thought as to how he'll measure up as a *husband*? Those are two very different roles, and they need to be regarded as such before you take that big step. Put another way, you may have liked the coming attraction, but how are you going to feel about the movie?

I suggest you take a year between the decision to marry and the actual wedding. Take another look at him just to be sure. You won't regret the extra effort.

Think about it: You learn something new every day. If you only learned last week that he has a bad habit of leaving his dirty socks on the bathroom floor every night, what other quirks can he be hiding? Nobody's perfect, of course, and we all have skeletons in our closets. Just make sure they're not real skeletons.

> Some people think of the engagement as the time to plan the wedding. I prefer to think of it as the time to plan the marriage. Use this period as more than a chance to show off your ring or choose the perfect cake. Take the opportunity to get to know—*really* get to know—your husband-to-be.

I know this can be a little anxious making, but use the engagement as a time to ask questions—of your fiancé and of yourself. Where do you want your life together to take you? These big questions may be somewhat impossible to answer in their large scale, so break them down and you'll be well on your way to knowing what's important in your marriage. Ask yourself, "*What would I be glad to know about him that it's impossible to know in the first few months of dating?*" Some information can truly only be gained with time.

Questions to Ask Each Other
Before You Say "I Do"

Do we want a large family or would we be content with just the two of us?

What role will spirituality or religious faith play in our lives?

Do we want an affluent lifestyle, or would we prefer a more modest standard of living, with more time to enjoy what makes us happy?

How will we manage our debts and savings?

Are there some things we are *not* prepared to give up in our marriage?

How do we feel about each other's families?

Why are we getting married? (You'd be surprised at how many people *don't* ask this all-important question.)

Are we prepared to face the challenges that marriage entails?

MARY JANE'S STORY

A friend of mine in her late thirties, Mary Jane, was keen to marry. She was an intelligent woman with a wonderful sense of humor, a gentle heart, and a life filled with love and friendship. Mary Jane was a librarian. Now, forget all those notions about the stern woman who shushes you from behind the stack of books—Mary Jane was beautiful, vivacious, and fun. She delighted in reading hour with the children, and you could count on her to recommend a good book or a scary movie. She also encouraged local writers, holding get-togethers where they could come and exchange ideas.

Mary Jane's days were lively and full. And yet, too often she would go home after work for a Lean Cuisine and a glass of wine. Mary Jane longed for a partner, someone she could share her day with, someone she could have fun with, someone who would be there in good times and bad. In short—a husband.

So Mary Jane did what a lot of women do these days: She went online. She was clear about the sort of person she was looking for, and she felt the best way to get an honest stand-up sort of guy was to be an honest, stand-up woman. She filled out her profile, resolving to tell the truth. She even mentioned her pet snake, Marmaduke.

LOVE IS PATIENT

Lesson One

Don't think waiting for marriage means being patient in the waiting—get out there and use modern technology to meet a good match.

Thirty-five dollars and four days later, Mary Jane had six dates lined up. *That was easy*, she thought. *I wonder why I hadn't done this before?* Six dates later she had her answer. Bachelor number one was too macho for her liking. Bachelor number two called his mother before their second martini. Mary Jane was willing to overlook bachelor number three's tattoos, but not the maniacal gleam in his eye. Bachelors four and five were no-shows, and bachelor number six, well, he turned out not to be a bachelor. Despite these setbacks, Mary Jane was determined to keep on trying. Her friends propped her up by laughing at her stories and giving her some much needed perspective.

"Honestly, Mary J," her friend Linda had said, "it's a numbers game, plain and simple. Just keep at it. He's out there somewhere. Promise."

"Easy for you to say," Mary Jane responded. "Whoever said all men are created equal obviously hasn't tried online dating."

But she kept at it. And then she met Tom. A successful businessman, Tom was not only charming and witty, he was the most attentive boyfriend she had ever had. He took her out to the theater and expensive restaurants. He called her two and three times a day, and was constantly sending her cute little text messages: luv u, c u 2night, ---<@ A rose 4 u cuz i luv u.

It was a whirlwind romance, but Mary Jane kept her head. She wanted to find someone who was good-natured and successful, someone who believed in the same values she did. Tom seemed to subscribe to those values. He worked hard. He had a generous nature, and he believed in something bigger than himself. Tom was exploring Buddhism, but he accompanied Mary Jane to her Mass every Sunday because, as he put it, "I want to know what's important to you."

It wasn't long before I received a phone call from Mary Jane asking me to officiate at their wedding. She was happy, and of course I was too. As her friend, I wanted to share in this moment with her, but as her counselor, I wanted to make sure she was making the right decision, so I asked to meet Tom. I was all set to like him. He seemed to fit the bill: smart, well spoken, respectful—almost too good to be true. I thought he was marriage material and that they stood a good chance of making a go of it. Nevertheless, I advised them to apply the brakes.

Follow your heart, but be quiet for a while first. Ask questions, look for the feelings behind the answers.

—UNKNOWN

"Why wait?" Tom asked. "We're adults. We know what we want."

Mary Jane, on the other hand, took my advice to slow down. Now on the threshold of the marriage that she had wanted for so long, she was able to take a good look at her life, where she had come from and where she was going.

Yes, she loved Tom.

Yes, she wanted to be married.

But she knew that the best way of making the marriage work was by making the engagement work. So, she insisted that Tom wait, because, as she said, "Before the rice is thrown and the toasts are made, I want to make sure I'm making the right decision. Sure, for the last few years I've thought a lot about getting married, but I have a good life and before I give it up I have to know that I'm moving toward something better—a real partnership. I love Tom, I really do. But I want to make sure we're right for each other. I want to believe in *this* marriage, not just the idea of marriage."

All went swimmingly for a time. Then gradually Tom changed. The man who was attentive became possessive. The man who was romantic became, at times, indifferent. He refused to mix with Mary Jane's friends, whom she loved to be with. This infuriated him and led to outbreaks of jealousy. Those once charming calls to check in with her became controlling, as he demanded to know where she was and who she was with, 24–7. Not that he told her where he was. Tom turned out to be a pathological liar who could not be trusted. His business was built on a mountain of debt, and more than once, Mary Jane had gone to the cash machine to find her checking account overdrawn. And his Buddhist exploration that had so impressed her? Turns out Tom wasn't exploring so much as he was dabbling; Buddhism was just the latest in a long line of religious experiments. Tom wasn't looking to discover a new way of looking at the world. He was just unable to commit to anything that made even the slightest demands on him.

Mary Jane was devastated. The man she had loved had never in fact existed. And yet, as hurt as she was, she was relieved, too. "Father Pat, if I hadn't insisted on a yearlong engagement I never would have known all these things," she confided. "Instead of a broken engagement, it would have been a broken marriage, and that would have been so much harder to bear."

LOVE IS PATIENT

Lesson Two

Have a yearlong engagement. Ask all the questions you can think of. You'll be glad you did.

After the split Mary Jane and I sat down to talk about her experiences and what she had learned from it all. As much as she needed a shoulder to cry on, she also needed someone to help her fit all the pieces together. After all, if you don't learn from the past, you won't grow.

"Tom was so charming, so handsome. He was everything I thought I wanted. I guess he was just too good to be true."

Talking it over, Mary Jane realized that she had ignored the red flags.

"He was very secretive," she told me. "I didn't press him. I mean, a relationship has to be based on trust, right?"

I agreed with her, but suggested that *informed*

trust, that is, trust based on real knowledge and experience of the other person, is much better than *blind trust,* which may have been closer to what was going on in this case.

Mary Jane agreed. "I guess I didn't ask enough questions about his past, period. I suppose, at first, I didn't care to know. We were in this perfect bubble where all that mattered was the here and now. It was so exhilarating. But after those first wonderful months, well, I started to notice things. His business? Well, I'm not an accountant, but there were a lot of tense phone calls, a lot of talk about cash flow, that sort of thing. It made me nervous.

"And when the wedding drew nearer, well, this whole 'for better or worse' thing became clear to me. I had fallen head over heels, but that seemed so long ago. Now whenever I was with Tom I just felt bad about myself. What was the point of that? What was the point of laying aside my old life (well, I thought of it then as my old life) for that? Why would I get married if what I was getting in return wasn't stronger, better? Something *more than* I had? You know?"

I did know.

TO PLEDGE, TO PROMISE, TO COMMIT

If there's anything that magazines and television shows have taught us, it's that men fear commitment. One young woman confided in me that the man she was seriously involved with had admitted his profound fear of commitment. He wanted to take some time apart and go to counseling on his own to explore his fears. She was a little nervous about this, understandably so. She was deeply in love with him and could not bear the prospect of a future without him. She worried that counseling might uncover something that would ultimately prevent their getting married, and that she would lose him.

That was a possibility, but there was another possibility too: that he would go to counseling and, through confronting his fears, overcome them. The very fact that this young man was able to discuss his fears with his girlfriend told me that he was a person of character, somebody who understood the importance of commitment even though he was frightened of it. This was a very good quality indeed.

LOVE IS PATIENT

Lesson Three

Getting married means you're making a sacred promise. That takes commitment... and commitment takes patience.

Make no mistake about it: Commitment is a frightening prospect for both men and women. It should be. The act of committing yourself to another person for the rest of your life is not one to be taken lightly. Marry in haste, repent in leisure, and all that. So if fear makes us take stock of our actions and if it makes us question not just our actions but our motives, it can be very useful.

I remember an incident from my seminary life. I must have been about twenty-seven. It was the eve of the day when my class of fifteen would be taking our final vows in the religious order I belong to. My roommate and good friend, let's call him Frank, was sitting on the windowsill of our room four stories up, looking more thoughtful than usual. He had sailed through the years of seminary life without a hitch. Now the moment of truth had come—and he looked worried.

"What's up, Frank?" said I.

He replied, "It's just dawned on me what we'll be doing tomorrow . . ."

In a moment of truth, he had to face the fact that he had never really thought about what he was getting into. Naturally enough, he was frightened.

That fear of commitment is natural, and in my experience, it seems that men fear commitment more than women. They worry that marriage will change them so they'll no longer be able to live by their own rules. Well, they're right. Marriage requires not just commitment, but compromise too. But for both these requirements—and they're big ones—a man who enters into marriage will get so much more than he gives up. He'll gain lifelong love, companionship, and support. He'll give and receive passion and friendship. There are even studies to show that married people are happier, healthier, and better off financially.

WARM HEART, COLD FEET

You should never put yourself in the position of trying to persuade your boyfriend to marry you. No good can come of that. If you want your boyfriend to be your life partner, but he has cold feet, well, you've got to face up to it. That means being clear on what you want both as individuals and as a couple. Talk it out with love and respect and, above all, honesty. And don't stall on the hard questions: What is he afraid of? And why?

> Patience is not just a virtue, it's a useful commodity for all aspects of life. And when it comes to marriage, patience is vital in helping you understand the complexities of committing your life to another person.

If commitment is hard for some men, it's because they have the idea it's the opposite of freedom, and that's what they value above all things. Many men are worried—terrified, might be more like it—that they are going to lose their independence. It's important to be patient with your boyfriend, but it's important to be realistic too. Women often make excuses for the men in their lives. "Oh, he's really busy," she'll say. "That's why he's so often late to pick me up." Or, "He's just frightened that his feelings for me are so deep." Unfortunately, women may try to soften the message to themselves in order to continue their relationship or prevent themselves from getting hurt. The irony here is that not all relationships should continue. And of course, there's no real way to prevent yourself from getting hurt. So whether he has a fear of commitment that he just can't get over—or to quote those now famous words "He's just not that into you . . ."—it's important for you to be realistic about your relationship and to pay attention to those actions that convey a lack of commitment on his part, whatever the reason.

Wedding **Bells** (OR) WARNING **Bells?**

↳ **How does he treat you?** *Talk is cheap* goes the expression. Your boyfriend may talk about love and commitment, but do his actions match his words? If, for example, he says you're the most important person in his life, then why doesn't he keep his promises to you? Respect or indifference—actions rarely lie.

↳ **How does he introduce you to others?** Does he present you as his girlfriend or his fiancée? Or does he use cloudy language that doesn't speak to the seriousness of your relationship? If he's reluctant to use the word *us,* or he introduces you as simply "my friend," he may not be ready for marriage.

↳ **How does he get on with your friends and family?** Is he keen to participate in your life and you in his? A marriage isn't just a joining of finances and furniture, it's the blending together of two lives and all the people who are in it. The man who is reluctant to get to know your friends (and have you get to know his) may not be the man you should marry.

COMMUNICATION IS KEY

If you've been thinking about premarital counseling, you may find yourself wondering if you and your fiancé should attend separately or together. The answer is simple: Both.

Marriage preparation programs can help cut through some of the anxiety you and your husband-to-be may be feeling. Hearing other couples discuss their relationships openly and honestly can give even the most reluctant mate the confidence to join in.

It's no surprise that men don't look forward to premarital counseling. I can tell if the husband-to-be has been dragged along to counseling by the scruff of his neck. He crosses his arms over his chest, examines the pictures on the wall of my office, or adopts some other posture that shows he is opposed to this conversation.

One bride recalled that her groom at first resisted premarital counseling until he looked around at the other couples in the class. Most of the couples were about their age, and though nearly all of the guys obviously did *not* want to be there, they were willing to try.

During one session I hosted, I remember asking a couple to profess what they loved about one another. Much to the woman's surprise, her fiancé opened up.

"I became emotional as he rattled off a lengthy list!" she recalled to me. "What really got to me was that he was able to say this out loud, when we weren't even alone."

Sometimes the hardest part about communication is breaking the seal. Once you're able to recognize your feelings for one another, you'll want to share them privately—and publicly. This will only help your compassion and understanding grow.

The next step in this open forum of communication is to voice what you do not like about your spouse-to-be, without being judgmental. You will be living with this person—if you keep those feelings bottled up they're likely to explode.

A young woman in one of my counseling sessions admitted that these less-than-positive observations were hard to hear. This was the same young woman who had glowed with delight at the long list of positives. "But when I was honest with myself, I agreed with his concerns, which I am now trying to address."

WISE WORDS FROM A MOTHER-IN-LAW

Communication isn't just about talking, it's about listening, too. And sometimes it's about *not* listening! Supreme Court Justice Ruth Bader Ginsburg shares these wise words from her mother-in-law. Ruth was dressing for her wedding when her mother-in-law-to-be came into the room and put something in Ruth's hand.

"I'm going to give you some advice that will serve you well," her mother-in-law said. "In every good marriage it pays sometimes to be a little deaf."

Ruth looked down at her hand to find a pair of wax earplugs. Writes Ginsburg: "Sometimes people say unkind or thoughtless things to you and, when they do, it's best to be a little hard of hearing—to

LOVE IS PATIENT

Lesson Four

In every good marriage it pays sometimes to be a little deaf.

tune out and not snap back in anger or impatience. In all my years of marriage I have recalled that advice regularly."

DETERMINED COMMUNICATION

When I meet with a couple who are thinking of marrying, I insist that they have a series of personal discussions with me. My sessions are based on a questionnaire.

I begin by asking the couple separately: "What's your definition of marriage—in twenty-five words or fewer?"

The first time I asked this question of a couple I was a little nervous. I half expected some tongue-in-cheek response like the one from the little boy who said that marriage "is when you like what she likes and so you live in the same house so you know where the chips and dip are kept." Or the little girl who said, "A man and woman get married so they can save money on the groceries."

I needn't have worried. The couples usually listen

intently. Very rarely does it happen that one of the partners shows no interest in the discussion. Most often the woman will begin. I'll only have to look at her and she fires off her definition.

And then I say, "What about you, Jack?"

Often "Jack" is flummoxed. Like a drowning man reaching for an oar, he repeats a different version of what his bride-to-be has said. And that's okay, because it shows that at some level he agrees with her. The word I look for, and it's amazing how often it comes first from the woman, is *commitment*. It's key.

How would your boyfriend define *commitment*, that crucial word in any discussion of marriage? I like to define commitment as "a sacred promise, freely chosen, to be devoted to another throughout your lives." Granted, there aren't many men who can come up with that. Some will say "it's about being there for each other" or "it's a decision to work together within and for our marriage." Often I'll hear something like "that's about 'till death do us part,' right?"

Don't worry if your intended has trouble coming up with a definition, especially on the first try. Men are often unable to voice their feelings, even though they may be deep and authentic. Don't expect him to open up all at once, and try not to get discouraged. Give him the opportunity to come around to the idea that while a relationship must be lived, sometimes it must be discussed, too. In other words, be patient.

Dear Father Pat

Dear Father Pat: I know my boyfriend loves me, but he never uses those three little words. Is that important? Signed: *Wanting Words*

Dear Wanting: Men are notoriously poor at talking about their feelings. Nevertheless, if a man is unable—or unwilling—to say "I love you," it can be a sign that he's not ready for marriage. Marriage is based on communication and commitment. If your intended cannot communicate his love, he may not be ready for the commitment.

COME WHAT MAY

Marriage is an open-ended commitment to an unpredictable person. On your wedding day you never know what lies ahead of you, and yet on The Day, you promise to stick by your partner come what may.

That's why the text of the traditional wedding ceremony includes those awesome words: "For better or for worse, in sickness and in health, for richer or poorer, till death do us part." Knees must tremble as those words are spoken.

You and your intended should go over that text carefully, word by word.

All of this brings up a much bigger issue. What you can do and *should* do, as far as your emotional and practical resources allow you to, is give your fiancé all the loving support you can with all the compassion you can muster. Remember: *patience*.

Compassion and patience are related, twin keys to unlocking the complexities of commitment. As for the pair grappling with the man's commitment issues, it is essential to keep probing the source of those feelings. Talking out the issue is the only way to resolve it. Question him as to what it is about commitment that scares him. Perhaps there's a history of divorce in his family. It's just possible that his fear of commitment might have its roots in some of your premarital behavior.

Ask him.

LOVE IS PATIENT

Lesson Five

Compassion and patience are related, twin keys to unlocking the complexities of commitment.

A CAUTIONARY TALE

Once, there was a blind date that nearly turned fatal.

The man and the woman, who had never met, were rushing in separate cars to make their dinner reservation at a popular restaurant. He was driving a Dodge Viper and she had a Volvo. The man went speeding through the stop sign and stopped dead short of colliding with her car.

Flustered and infuriated, he rolled down his window and let loose with a barrage of threats and suggestions.

"Leave it to a woman to almost wreck my car!" he yelled.

He iced the cake of his remark with an additional comment that had nothing to do with her driving.

Each parked their car, and she made a special effort to park as far from his vehicle as possible. The restaurant was crowded, so each waited at the bar unobserved by one another, until the table was called.

It wasn't until the moment the host seated them that each recognized the other as their stop-sign foe. Their expressions displayed a mixture of fear and embarrassment, and a silence ensued for what seemed like forever. Finally, they simultaneously burst into laughter.

The woman was at a loss for words. However, the man thought quickly and came up with a quip. "I'm sorry," he stuttered. "I was talking to the person in the car behind you."

There was no second date.

An overwhelming number of young men and women admit to looking for a "soul mate" in marriage—that one person you'll meet while the tenor sings "Some Enchanted Evening," and who alone will fulfill

LOVE IS PATIENT

Lesson Six

If he is consistently impatient, with you and with others, move on.

all your needs. You will know instinctively that he is The One. When you look at him across the crowded room, your knees turn to jelly. If you can only snare him, you won't need anyone else in your life except the perfect children you'll have with him. You might have to wait patiently for the appearance of this soul mate, but so what. You'll know him when you see him, and he'll know you.

The trouble with this soul mate scenario is that it's unrealistic. For one thing, the term *soul mate* implies that there is only one person out there who can fulfill your desire for a loving relationship. There are many such prospective partners, each with his own virtues, and it's up to you to discern who is going to be the best marriage partner *over the long term*.

The choice is yours; never forget that. It's up to you to choose a *mate* from the many *soul mates* out there.

Whomever you choose, understand that on your long road together there may be some other surprises, like a couple of sharp corners. For one thing, either you or your husband may come across some so-called "soul mates" even after you have married. Bear this in mind, and remind yourself that no "soul mate" is as important as your "mate" or your marriage. While you may enter into your relationship as man and woman, it is marriage itself—and your active and loving participation in it—that will make you husband and wife.

And for another thing—and this happens to us all—there will come a day when you realize that your partner, *soul mates* though you are, is an imperfect being. Some days the disappointments will be minor, like leaving the cap off the toothpaste, while other days the challenges will be much greater. That's why it's so important to take your time in choosing the right partner, and to understand that the choice is yours. Follow every doubt you have and don't commit until you feel certain he's the one you want to marry. Consider this:

He may turn your knees to jelly—but does he

want to go to bed with you the first time you meet him?

He may be smashingly handsome and sexy, but is he a drug addict?

He may ooze charm from every pore, but is he truthful?

Your friends may admire you for being sought after by this paragon—but what are his goals in life?

Maybe your prospective soul mate will answer these questions and other tough ones—then you might tentatively decide to begin to cultivate his companionship—using your head at *all* times.

You have to kiss a lot of frogs to find a prince.

LOVE IS PATIENT

Lesson Seven

Stop looking for your soul mate. Mr. Perfect is not out there!

The Seven Lessons of
Love Is Patient

1. Don't think waiting for marriage means being patient in the waiting—get out there and use modern technology to meet a good match.

2. Have a yearlong engagement. Ask all the questions you can think of. You'll be glad you did.

3. Getting married means you're making a sacred promise. That takes commitment... and commitment takes patience.

4. In every good marriage it pays sometimes to be a little deaf.

5. Compassion and patience are related, twin keys to unlocking the complexities of commitment.

6. If he is consistently impatient, with you and with others, move on.

7. Stop looking for your soul mate. Mr. Perfect is not out there!

THREE

Love Is Kind

KINDNESS IS FOUND IN ALL
GOOD AND LOVING RELATIONSHIPS

We know kindness when we see it. We know that it lives in the little things—a door held open, a sympathetic word, a caring smile. We extend kindness to others when we help them bear their burdens and when we simply listen. Kindness is found in the story of the Good Samaritan, in the works of the Dalai Lama, and in all good and loving relationships.

Kindness means, amongst other things, listening to another with an open heart and mind. It means showing respect and paying attention. Kindness understands what another person needs, and is able to respond with generosity, compassion, and tenderness. Above all, kindness recognizes another person's humanity. Cultivate kindness in your life and in your relationships, and you will plant the seeds of kindness in your marriage.

LOVE IS KIND

Lesson One

Cultivate kindness in your life and you will plant the seeds of kindness in your marriage.

THINK!

Think before you speak, the minister Thomas Tuell always said, and he came up with this lovely rubric to help us remember. In all you have said or are about to say, ask yourselves these questions:

T stands for "Is it TRUE?"

H stands for "Is it HELPFUL?"

I is for "Is it INSPIRING?"

N stands for "Is it NECESSARY?"

K stands for "Is it KIND?"

I urge couples to put this word THINK on their refrigerator door. In fact, I like to imagine newlyweds moving into their new home and looking at their refrigerator door to guard their tongues when they are speaking with one another: true, helpful, inspiring, necessary, and kind.

HEATHER'S STORY
....

Heather met Ross at a party. She had just come off a bad breakup with her boyfriend of three years, and was more than a little bruised. The party was Heather's first attempt at reclaiming her social life, but she went reluctantly and only because her friend Emma had pried her out of her apartment.

"Enough," Emma had said. "You're carrying this Miss Havisham act too far. It's time to get on with it and get back out there."

Now there's a good friend.

Heather was a young musician who was often described as offbeat. She had a few tattoos, a quirky sense of humor, and a great love of adventure—not to mention chocolate. Ross, a trial lawyer new to town, was handsome in a clean-cut sort of way, but he seemed a little too conventional for Heather. Still, she took Emma's advice and gave Ross her number when he asked for it.

Their first date—dinner and a movie—was lovely. Ross took Heather to his favorite Indian restaurant, and she took him to an old, out-of-the-way cinema where they watched a Marx Brothers movie. Their second date, brunch and a walk through the park, was even better. Heather talked about her love of music, and Ross shared his passion for the law. They exchanged stories about their childhoods, and Heather even laughed at Ross's incredibly corny jokes. Despite all this, Heather was holding back. She couldn't resist the urge to compare Ross to her last boyfriend, who had been much more exciting. Plus, she was finding it hard to get over the whole "lawyer thing." But he was a nice guy and she was determined to give it a try.

Now it was time for that all-important third date and Ross suggested a drive in the country.

It was one of those lovely September days when the weather was just beginning to change. The sun was shining and a gentle breeze was blowing as they strolled through the streets, taking in the picturesque nineteenth-century architecture and looking at antique shops. On a whim, they stopped to sample the ice cream at the local sweets parlor where they both ordered two scoops of double fudge chocolate.

Suddenly, a commotion arose outside.

A young boy exiting the shop, ice cream cone in hand, had been grazed by a hit-and-run driver.

The boy was scared but still standing. Bystanders had taken down the car's license plate number, but were milling around, unsure how to act.

Ross took command of the situation. He gently guided the little boy back into the parlor and looked him over to make sure he wasn't badly hurt. He got another ice cream cone for the child, whose name was Peter, and even cracked a joke or two to cheer him up. He called the boy's mother on his cell phone, and waited until the police arrived.

Heather looked on in admiration. Ross hadn't panicked. He had taken control of the situation and seemed to know instinctively what needed to be done. But more than that, Ross had treated the boy with such kindness, almost as if he were his own son. Heather was touched beyond words at this man's character. She saw in his gentleness a tremendous strength. That one episode showed her the depth of kindness in his heart. It showed Heather who Ross was. Perhaps more importantly, it showed Heather what she wanted.

LOVE IS KIND

Lesson Two

Be kind by being sensitive to the needs of others.

KINDNESS LISTENS

Does your partner pay attention? Does he really listen to you? Even in love, we too often neglect kindness; it seems we make up excuses to avoid it: a bad day at work, a night without sleep. Sometimes we're too concerned with our own affairs, thoughts, plans, and distractions to consider the other person.

One of the best ways we show kindness is by listening. Unfortunately, we're not that good at it. I remember a story that Walter Cronkite, the famous CBS newsman, told in *Around America,* his recollections of people and places along America's seashores.

LOVE IS KIND

Lesson Three

Show kindness by listening.

He loved sailing. On this particular day he was sailing along the Mystic River in Connecticut. As his sailboat, *Wyntje*, was passed by another vessel, the young people on board were calling out, "Hello, Walter! Hello, Walter!" Walter was delighted that he was remembered and recognized.

So he doffed his yachting cap and waved. As his sloop got closer to the other vessel, the cries of the crew redoubled: "Hello, Walter! Hello, Walter!" He bowed to them and waved.

"I waved back a cheery greeting," Cronkite recalled, "and my faithful mate [his wife, Betsy] said, 'What do you think they were shouting?'

" 'Why, "Hello, Walter," ' I replied.

" 'No,' she said. 'They were shouting a warning, "Low water!" ' "

He heard what he wanted to hear.

What I realize as I get older is that Michelle is less concerned about me giving her flowers than she is about me doing things that are hard for me—carving out time. That to her is proof, evidence that I'm thinking about her. She appreciates the flowers, but to her romance is that I'm actually paying attention to things that she cares about, and time is always an important factor.

—PRESIDENT BARACK OBAMA

Too often we see things not as *they* are, but as *we* are. That's what one young man found out. The relationship he had formed with his girlfriend was developing, and the man was considering marriage. To make certain there was nothing in the woman's past that would embarrass him, he hired a detective agency to run a check on her. The agency assigned an agent who was not told the client's identity.

When the agent reported back, he said, "The young lady is a splendid person, except for one unfortunate blemish. Lately, she's been dating a businessman of questionable reputation."

Indeed.

MY COMPLIMENTS

Does he pay you compliments often or not at all? Is he always putting you in a favorable light when you are with others? Or does he criticize you in front of other people, making fun of you and your cherished ideas, tastes, or opinions?

"My fiancé," one woman told me, "often belittles me in front of our friends. He says he loves me and just wants to help me become a better person. How can I convince him to save his criticisms for our private times?"

In all human relationships we should pay attention to what people do rather than what they say. This woman's fiancé says he loves her, but his behavior, belittling her in front of her friends, says otherwise.

> Never marry a man who doesn't pay you compliments.

I am at a loss to understand how his belittling her can help her to become a better person, as he claims. There are few more devastating things that one human being can do to another than belittle the other in public. Most of us have fragile egos, easily crushed. Her fiancé would be better off praising her in front of others rather than belittling her. Even Homer Simpson can come up with a compliment: "Marge, you're as pretty as Princess Leia and as smart as Yoda," he told his long-suffering wife.

If your fiancé is not able to pay you a compliment—if he doesn't come up to the standards set by Homer Simpson—*don't marry him!*

Dear Father Pat

Dear Father Pat: My boyfriend has a stressful job that makes a lot of demands on him. I respect that, and understand that he has to work a lot. But even when we're together, well, he'll be checking his BlackBerry™ or talking on his cell phone with clients. Should I just shrug it off? Signed: *Neglected*

Dear Neglected: Paying attention is another way we show love, so if your boyfriend is falling short in that department, it's time for *you* to pay attention. Sit down and talk to your boyfriend—or send him an e-mail or call him on his BlackBerry™—and tell him how you feel about the situation. Chances are he'll give you some nice words to make you feel better. That's fine, but if those words aren't followed up with action, it's time to walk away.

P.S.: Be careful about the things you shrug off in your premarital relationship. It might not be so easy to shrug them off in your marriage.

TEACH A MAN TO FISH

Empathy is a big part of kindness. It's the unique ability to feel the experiences, needs, aspirations, frustrations, sorrows, joys, anxieties, hurt, or hunger of another as if they were your own. Empathy means putting your ear to another's heart and asking, "Who are you, really? What do you need?"

Everyone knows that wonderful old Chinese proverb, "Give a man a fish and he'll eat for a day. Teach a man to fish and he'll eat for a lifetime." Perhaps you even know some of the variations: Teach a man to fish and you can sell him fishing equipment; Teach a man to fish and if he doesn't like sushi, then you'll also have to teach him to cook; and Teach a man to fish and he'll sit in the boat and drink beer all day.

Well, there's a version of this story that I love, and it has nothing to do with drinking beer. A little boy went fishing with his grandmother while his parents were away on vacation, or so the story goes. The first grader was equipped with a toy fishing rod with a plastic hook that wouldn't really have caught anything, but his hopes were high, as were his spirits. He was spending the day with his beloved grandmother, and they were going fishing!

To the pond they went. Now, this pond may have been beautiful in a storybook kind of way—deep blue waters surrounded by lush green trees—but it was devoid of any fish. They may as well have gone fishing in the bathtub. Nevertheless, the boy and his grandmother had a lovely afternoon. Granny shared some old stories with her grandson, who in turn delighted her with his favorite knock-knock jokes. Together they enjoyed a picnic basket of peanut butter sandwiches, chocolate milk, and Granny's homemade Rice Krispies squares. It would have been a perfect day if not for one thing: no fish.

The boy was as patient as a first grader could be, and he tried to hide his disappointment when, after a couple of hours, his grandmother said it was time to go home. As they settled into the drive home, the child looked dejectedly out the window at the stream that paralleled the roadside. His grandmother, realizing the depths of the boy's despair, pulled up in front of a delicatessen and asked the boy to wait for just a moment while she went inside.

Whenever possible, be kind.
It is always possible.

—THE DALAI LAMA

As she got back into the car, she said, "I have a feeling you're going to catch a fish today after all."

In the kitchen, she put a large pot on the table, and emptied the contents of the white deli bag—three smoked whitefish. She handed the boy his fishing pole, and said, "Now you'll see how good a fisherman you really are."

I hope this boy's future wife has an opportunity to thank this kind granny, because her empathy—her ability to look at this small child and put herself in his position—helped bring about in this boy the self-respect to stand tall in the world.

Teach him to fish indeed.

LOVE IS KIND

Lesson Four

Empathy puts its ear to another's heart and asks, "Who are you, really? What do you need?"

CHERISH THE GOOD

The definition of kindness is a broad one. I'd say it includes looking for the good in all the ordinary dealings with a partner. Rather than thinking about problems and annoyances, dwell on the good times and good qualities. In the gallery of our minds we can choose to hang memories of unhappiness and gloom or we can hang pictures of peaceful, caring times. Choosing to remember and cherish the good makes a big difference in the quality of the relationship, so practice kindness in equal parts action and emotion.

Practice Kindness

Write a heartfelt letter to your partner.

Make him feel as if he is a welcome presence in your life.

Show interest in his well-being.

Tell him what you like about him (even if it's hard to think of a particular quality that day).

Do something special for someone you love every day.

As tempting as it may be to succumb to petty grievances (behavior most often motivated by the selfish urge to be "right"), use kindness as a means to communicate.

Be watchful for—and engage in—spontaneous demonstrations of kindness. They can happen most unexpectedly, yet reveal so much. The husband who returns his wife's library book (and pays the fine!) and the wife who unexpectedly picks her husband up

LOVE IS KIND

Lesson Five

Choose to remember and cherish the good.

from his late meeting—they both know the value of a kind and loving gesture. They know the value of their relationship.

Don't forget magnanimity, which is something larger and deeper than generosity. What a marvelous virtue that is. Magnanimity, which is very much about fair-mindedness, means appreciating a partner's strengths, even when his weaknesses come to the fore. It means a daily determination to give more than what may be needed—willingly and gladly.

When I was in high school, we used to play Rugby. The members of the varsity team came together once a year to elect a captain for the next season. We were all seventeen or eighteen.

One of the boys had repeated his senior year at

Marriage Advice

*Let your love be stronger than your
hate and anger.
Learn the wisdom of compromise,
for it is better to bend a little
than to break.
Believe the best rather than the worst.
People have a way of living up or down
to your opinion of them.
Remember that true friendship is the
basis for any lasting relationship.
The person you choose to marry
is deserving of the courtesies and
kindnesses you bestow on your friends.
Please hand this down to your children
and your children's children.*

—JANE WELLS

(1886)

school, only because he wanted to be captain of the Rugby team. It didn't work out, though. *I* was elected captain. I can still see him, sitting in the classroom, his hopes dashed. Yet he came over to shake my hand. That act had an enormous impact on me. The very reason he came back didn't work out, but he stayed on for the year and helped us win every game in sight. That's magnanimity.

BE KIND TO YOURSELF

If you're like most women, you take tremendous care to be kind to your partner. But do you treat yourself with the same kindness? Do you listen to yourself with an open heart? Are you paying attention?

Ask yourself the question "Why have I decided to marry him?" Take some time to be quiet and look inward. Be true to yourself—be kind—and answer honestly. You may not get the answer you were expecting.

I make a point of asking the men and women who come to see me for premarital counseling why they are getting married. Most responses are beautiful and informed by insight. Some, however, are problematic:

- ⌐ *I'm marrying to get out of living with my parents.*
- ⌐ *I'm marrying him because he's rich.*
- ⌐ *I'm marrying because I don't want to be alone.*
- ⌐ *I'm marrying because I'm pregnant.*
- ⌐ *I'm marrying to rescue him; his life will be in shambles if I don't. (Obviously this woman hadn't heard this advice from Mae West: "Don't marry a man to reform him. That's what reform schools are for.")*

Couples who marry for less-than-ideal reasons will regret their decision. It's as I heard once: Marriage is like a cafeteria. You take what looks good to you and pay for it later.

LOVE IS KIND

Lesson Six

Ask each other the question "Why have I decided to marry you?" Be sure you are comfortable with the answers.

Why Did You Get Married?

Simply a case of logic. We loved each other and wanted to build a family together.—Keri S.

He's the kindest man I have ever known. —Betsy F.

I was swept off my feet. And that wasn't easy—I'm clumsy!—Karen B.

He makes me laugh.—Ellen R.

I couldn't imagine my life without him. —Gretchen T.

He's my best friend.—Jenny T.

It was love at first sight. That was twenty-five years ago!—Keesha W.

He believed in me.—Monica F.

We wanted the same things out of life. —Lucy R.

I liked the shape of his neck.—My mother, Patricia Margaret

A FRIEND INDEED

Is kindness among the qualities you admire in your future husband? I hope so. And I hope you take the opportunity to consider what other qualities you admire in him, too.

You may admire a quality in him that has nothing to do with being successfully married to him—like charm, or being a good storyteller, or being the life of the party, or being a Democrat or a Republican! But be on the lookout for those qualities that will make a good husband. Is he a good listener? Is he adaptable, loyal, and kind? Is he your friend?

The couple who cultivates friendship enjoys one another's company; they respect one another's opinions; they do all kinds of things together. Are you happier when your partner is near? If the answer is yes, *here* is a man to consider.

"When you meet the right man, you will know," a happily married woman told me. "My husband and I met playing on a baseball team for work. It was a big deal for charity, and even though it was supposed to be a fun day out of the office, everybody was tense and competitive. Well, he was the pitcher and I played second base. He was a great player and I was pretty good, but not good enough apparently. I flubbed a ball in the ninth and blew the game. Well, I felt awful, letting the team down, but my now-husband could see how bad I was feeling and he came right over to console me. He made some corny joke about getting to second base, and from then on we were friends. We built our relationship from there."

LOVE IS KIND

Lesson Seven

Friendship is the solid ground upon which marriage is built.

The Seven Lessons of
Love Is Kind

1. Cultivate kindness in your life and you will plant the seeds of kindness in your marriage.

2. Be kind by being sensitive to the needs of others.

3. Show kindness by listening.

4. Empathy puts its ear to another's heart and asks, "Who are you, really? What do you need?"

5. Choose to remember and cherish the good.

6. Ask each other the question "Why have I decided to marry you?" Be sure you are comfortable with the answers.

7. Friendship is the solid ground upon which marriage is built.

FOUR

Love Is Not Envious or Boastful or Arrogant or Rude

 Dear Father Pat

Dear Father Pat: I love dancing, but my boyfriend always declines my offers to dance with me. When I'm dancing with other boys, I can feel him staring at us. How can I help him to like dancing and to stop staring? Signed: *Not Dancing with the Stars*

Dear Not Dancing: You'll probably never get your boyfriend to like dancing, and the staring probably means that jealousy is in play here. Have a chat with him about that unlovely quality. If he persists in his jealousy-laden behavior, drop him!

THE GREEN-EYED MONSTERS

Envy and jealousy are as complex as they are puzzling. And they're both destructive.

Envy is pain at the good fortune of others. An often intense feeling, envy produces displeasure and resentment on seeing the success, advantage, or prosperity of another. It can color everything and overshadow even the happiest moment. For the person governed by envy, a compliment to one person is an insult to himself.

Envy is a cruel motivator and the most useless of all the vices. It brings no pleasure. It only corrodes your spirit.

Envy is the art of counting the other fellow's blessings instead of your own.

—HAROLD COFFIN

It's important to distinguish between *envy* and *jealousy*. *Envy* is a solo act; *jealousy* is a threesome.

Jealousy is a negative emotion fueled by the fear of loss. A jealous person believes he must guard what he is most at risk of losing, and he is often consumed by thoughts of this loss—real or imagined. Jealousy stirs the imagination and makes us think the worst. It can be unreasonable and irrational, and it can destroy even the strongest relationships. Jealousy causes distress, both to the person who feels it and the person who is the object of it.

Jealousy is a dangerous ingredient in any relationship because it can take away your freedom to live a free, responsible life. You can't live and love fully if someone is jealous of you or if you are jealous of someone else.

LOVE IS NOT
ENVIOUS

Lesson One

Envy and jealousy are dangerous ingredients in any relationship.

LISA'S STORY

Lisa and Jeff were one of those couples who were meant to be together. Everybody said so. They hadn't been dating very long—only four months—but they were inseparable. Public displays of affection were the norm for this young couple. They were always holding hands, quick to kiss and embrace. They went on several dates a week and not a day went by without a flurry of e-mails, text messages, and phone calls.

One evening at a party, Jeff went to the bar for drinks when he noticed that Lisa was dancing with another man. He paused to see what would happen when the music stopped. The two of them—Lisa and her new friend—sat down at the table together to chat. The new man leaned in closer to whisper into her ear; she giggled at whatever he'd said. They seemed quite chummy. Lisa even put her hand on his shoulder affectionately.

That's when Jeff felt his blood pressure rising.

He flew into a jealous rage, tossing the drinks onto the floor and storming over to the table.

"This is unbelievable!" he screamed, arms waving. "Lisa—what's going on here? I walk away for one minute, and you find someone else. I *knew* you couldn't be trusted!"

Lisa looked up at him, still somehow maintaining her composure, and said, "I'd like you to meet my cousin."

She told Jeff it was over, then left the party.

*Jealousy is all the fun
you think they had.*

—ERICA JONG

Jeff pursued her for days after, begging her forgiveness and offering heartfelt apologies.

"Lisa," he pleaded, "I'm so very sorry. I was an idiot. A real idiot. It's just that I love you so much. I couldn't stand the thought of losing you. I don't know what came over me."

"Jeff," she reasoned, "you didn't trust me. I was across the room from you and you didn't think you could trust me that far? What am I to make of that?"

"I know . . . I know . . . ," he countered. "It's just that, well, you looked so beautiful that night. I was so proud of you . . . and that guy. Well, he's really good-looking and I hadn't seen him before. Lisa . . . oh, Lisa . . . it just all caved in. I've never felt like this before. About anyone. The feelings, well, they scared me."

It went on like that for days. Lisa was angry, then she was sad. She was worried, too, about seeing this new side of the man she was falling in love with. But she missed him—the way he made her laugh, the way he made her feel. Anybody can make a mistake, she reasoned. If I love him, shouldn't I forgive him?

So Lisa and Jeff got back together. Lisa saw a little evidence of his jealousy from time to time—a few too many questions when she was out with friends, for example—but she could see that Jeff was trying very hard to behave in the way he knew he should and there was never another incident. Still, when they decided to get married some months later, Lisa insisted they come to see me. She wanted to make sure she and Jeff had a strong relationship. She wanted to make sure they supported each other and that when things got tough there wasn't a repeat performance of the earlier incident.

> *Jealousy is to a relationship*
> *what wind is to rock—it can*
> *wear it away over time.*

"This is where your spirituality kicks in," I told them for openers. "And it's where the preacher in me kicks in too, I have to say."

At this Lisa looked a little worried, as if I were going to suggest we get on our knees and pray. I told her to relax, that they were clear on that front until the next Sunday. Then I launched into what I hoped wasn't a lecture.

"I believe that we are all made in the image and likeness of God," I said. "That's the truth of who we are, and it's a powerful one. That truth of our being contains a drumroll of attributes, and those attributes—like love—can be expressed in a largeness of heart that trumps envy and jealousy."

Jeff and Lisa looked a little puzzled.

"Okay, I can see that I'm losing you," I said. "Not

to worry. That little speech is like my old car. Sometimes it works. Sometimes it doesn't."

> Never marry a man who can't keep his jealousy in check.

I decided to take a more secular approach. I told them about a couple I'd just counseled who had dealt with similar issues of jealousy and envy. The husband made friends very easily—with women as well as men—and this caused the wife a great deal of distress. It wasn't that she didn't trust him. It's that she wished she had that same talent for friendship. That was envy talking. When she opened up a little more she confessed she was worried that her husband might find one of these women more interesting and attractive than her. That was jealousy.

Her husband was shocked at what she said and felt sorry he had hurt her in this unintended way. The wife felt better for voicing her fears. She was surprised, too, that just talking about her jealousy made her feel better. That was the first step. Once the husband understood that his new friendships were threatening to his wife, he agreed not to expand his circle of women friends. This couple understood that envy and jealousy were a problem in their relationship, and they committed to working through it together. That was the second step.

Lisa and Jeff had a head start, as they had already addressed Jeff's jealousy between themselves. They came back for several sessions, during which the three of us explored not just the roots of Jeff's fear, but the nature of jealousy itself. Lisa was trying to understand it, while Jeff was trying to overcome it. Jeff realized that jealousy may create rivals where none exist. Moreover, he realized how destructive jealousy was to the trust in their relationship. Jeff and Lisa

LOVE IS NOT
ENVIOUS

Lesson Two

Feelings aren't right or wrong in themselves. It's what you do with them that counts.

worked on this problem with dedication and love. And when they understood that there is no emotion that can't be redeemed, that feelings aren't right or wrong in themselves, that it's what you do with them that counts, I knew they were well on their way to building the happy marriage they both wanted.

KEEPING UP WITH THE JONESES

A young married man had just landed a job as an architect. It was his first professional job after graduating, and it was a very big deal indeed. He was keen to excel in his new career, and keen to impress his new colleagues too. Seems his ego had grown along with his skills, however, and soon he was urging his wife to sell the family clunker for something flashier.

"An architect should have a car that makes a personal statement," he said, "and our car makes us look stodgy and conventional and poor."

His wife laughed. "Well, I don't know about stodgy and conventional, but those student loans have put us pretty close to poor."

> *Envy is a useless vice. Its satisfaction*
> *is short-lived. It doesn't give you*
> *any pleasure, and it doesn't rejoice*
> *in the success of others.*

"No one will take me seriously if they see me driving around in it."

His wife tried to talk him out of buying the car. She reminded him not just of their student loans, but of their agreement to save for a down payment on a house. The car was a low third on their list of priorities. But he persisted.

"C'mon, honey," he cooed, "let's trade up."

She relented.

The pleasure of the vehicle, however, was short-lived. The satisfaction her husband derived from the new car led to a desire for new clothes, a bigger apartment, and frequent nights out at the latest hot spots. It was a glamorous life, but it wasn't the life the young couple had embarked on together. At least that's what the wife thought. She tried to talk to her husband about it. "Sweetheart," she said, "I married one man and you're becoming another. I don't understand what you want anymore."

"Oh, that's not true," he protested. "I just want us to have what we deserve in life."

"What we deserve is a loving and happy marriage, a future with children, and a home. You used to be motivated by that. Now . . ."—and here she teared

Dear Father Pat

Dear Father Pat: My boyfriend's favorite activity is shopping for expensive clothes. Then he wants to go to pricey restaurants to show them off. I prefer eating at home and wearing my comfortable clothes. How can I change him to like the simpler life? Signed: *On a Budget*

Dear On a Budget: Change him? Forget it! He's a bad risk for marriage. I'm afraid it's just that simple.

up—"you seem to be motivated by nothing but envy, by this perverse desire to keep up with the Joneses."

Her husband listened, he even tried to defuse the situation with a bad joke about preferring to keep up with the Smiths, but in the end he didn't really hear. He didn't change his profligate ways, nor did he realize how much his envy had damaged him and his relationship. And then it was too late. The marriage ended in divorce.

HARD TO SAY I'M SORRY

In the seventies—this would be the 1970s and not, as some of you may think, the 1870s—there was a blockbuster movie called *Love Story*. A tearjerker if ever there was one, *Love Story* followed the model of *boy meets girl, boy gets girl, girl dies a tragic death, boy mourns lost love*. *Love Story* made a great impression on moviegoers the world over and not just because of the extravagant tragedy of its plot. *Love Story* was infinitely popular because of a catchy little phrase: "Love means never having to say you're sorry." When Ali MacGraw uttered those words, something seemed to shift in the world. I can't tell you the number of times people repeated those words to each other with the deepest sincerity and belief. *Love means never having to say you're sorry.* To which I would say: *NONSENSE!*

> Never marry a man who doesn't know how to apologize.

IN THE DOGHOUSE

Is the man you're getting serious about able to say "I was wrong"?

During her engagement, a woman adopted a puppy. Her fiancé came over to her house to meet the little dog, and he came up with the idea of building a doghouse for the backyard.

"Honey," he said, "this doghouse will match the exterior of your home perfectly, and it will be the envy of the neighborhood. Tomorrow I'll go to the hardware store and buy the materials."

That weekend, he set up shop in the basement and began construction.

"It's such a big house for such a little dog," she said.

"You'll see," he reassured her. "I'm building it to scale."

"Honey," she gently urged, "are you sure it's not going to be too big?"

He gave her a look that said *I know what I'm doing,* so she left him to his own devices.

Within a week or so, the project was completed. Boy, was it beautiful: White wood with black shutters and a red door, it did indeed mirror his fiancée's house. The couple excitedly made preparations to transfer the house outdoors. They carted it carefully up the basement stairs to exit through the back. It wasn't until they pushed it to the door that they realized the house was too large to fit through. They tried every

LOVE IS NOT
ENVIOUS

Lesson Three

Sometimes love needs to say "I'm sorry."

which way to extricate the doghouse from the cellar, but it was no use. The house was simply too big. The groom-to-be had no choice but to admit he had made a major mistake by not measuring the doorway.

"I'm sorry," he simply offered. Then they both fell about laughing.

That doghouse has become something of a joke for the young couple, a symbol of both wrongheadedness and forgiveness. Whenever the husband or wife does something wrong, it's not uncommon for them to look at the other and say with a smile, "I guess I'm in the doghouse, eh?"

SACRED INDEPENDENCE

Love is not proud.

The humble person does not see himself as the sun around which all the other planets revolve, but tries to see every other person in his or her sacred independence. You don't need to know that I'm quoting former Secretary General of the UN Dag Hammarskjöld to know that there's a mountain of truth in that phrase *sacred independence*.

It's worth considering these words separately in order to come closer to their beauty and strength. We all know *sacred* as a word that's closely associated with God and religion, meaning something dedicated to a religious or spiritual purpose. With my being a priest, well, that's what you would expect. But *sacred* can also mean something worthy of your dedication. Think about it: Your dedication to your friends, your family, your job, can all be sacred in their meaning and application. As for *independence?* That's the icing on the wedding cake here, because being independent means not being subject to someone else's authority or control. That means each one of us is equal to the other, no matter what our circumstances.

Nuptial Blessing

May your husband put his trust in you and recognize that you are his equal and the heir with him to the life of grace.

There's a lovely story about Gandhi arriving at a village in India by train during the time he was leading Indians in their struggle to wrest independence from the British. At one end of the platform stood the dignitaries of the town, properly accoutered. Cordoned off at the other end of the platform were the Untouchables.

You can guess what happened. Gandhi ignored the dignitaries and walked straight toward the Untouchables, each one of whom he saw in their "sacred independence." He called them "Harijans"—children of God. Only after he had paid his respects to the Harijans did he make for the dignitaries, whom, we can be sure, he saw also in their sacred independence.

The first of earthly blessings—
independence.

—EDWARD GIBBON

Think of how this applies to your relationship. You are two separate but equal parties who have, of your own love and free will, dedicated yourselves to each other. You are still your own person—very much so—but you are also part of something larger than yourself, a marriage you have created out of desire and devotion. Can you think of anything more sacred than that?

> *Be patient toward all that is unsolved in your heart. And try to love the questions themselves.*
>
> —RAINER MARIA RILKE

CLARK KENT OR SUPERMAN?

The word *humility* sometimes gets a bad reputation in this modern world. It conjures up images of Clark Kent, not Superman, of nice guys who finish last. Nothing could be further from the truth. The humble person may still be confident; in fact, he often is! The humble person knows who he is and does not feel the need to cloak himself in arrogance.

LOVE IS NOT
ENVIOUS

Lesson Four

Beware of cultivating a relationship with a man who is not humble.

The humble person makes use of the art of conversation as one of the ways to discover the true nature of another. "The apt and cheerful conversation of man with woman is the chief and noblest purpose of marriage," the newlywed John Milton wrote.

Is the man you love able to engage in "apt and cheerful conversation"? His answers will reveal much. Whether he's humble or not, these exploratory talks are, or should be, fascinating experiences. What does your boyfriend think of humility? Does your boyfriend try to see you in your "sacred independence"?

RULES ARE MADE TO BE BROKEN

A lot of men and women adhere to theories and rules in their dating lives. The rules—and I've heard some harsh ones—take into account anything from who calls whom and when, who pays for dinner, and how many dates to have before either becoming intimate or moving on.

> *Compromise is the essence of diplomacy; and diplomacy is the cornerstone of love.*
>
> —UNKNOWN

I'm uncomfortable with this rules approach to dating, especially in the early days of a relationship. Rules and regulations are rigid, and they may not take into account the other's feelings. Moreover, rules can quickly morph into ultimatums, and that's not good for anybody. Rules also encourage a games approach to dating that pits him against her/her against him, and may also discourage men and women from looking at each new relationship as a fresh possibility.

A woman in a premarital counseling course once told me about her dating philosophy. "I had this three-month theory in college," she explained. "It was just one of those things I observed for myself. After three months things begin to fall apart."

A theory? I wondered. *Or a self-fulfilling prophecy?*

She continued. "I also made it a rule never to even offer to contribute to dinner on the first three dates. And I never called him for the first month."

"Which made things difficult," her fiancé added. "I lost my cell phone with her number in it and had to track her down through her lab partner."

He continued, moving on to the subject of men's dating "regulations."

"How often do you hear rules like if you get some girl's number, you are supposed to wait three days to call her? You know . . . so as not to seem too interested," he explained.

"Or desperate!" his fiancée added.

"If I got a girl's number," he continued, "did that mean I was supposed to call her that day? The next

**LOVE IS NOT
ENVIOUS**

Lesson Five

Rules are good servants but
bad masters.

day? I got all confused. You don't want to appear vulnerable. You don't want to appear needy."

But when does the notion of *not being needy* deny your needs? And when does this *not being needy* turn into rudeness?

Rules can become rudeness when one does not treat the other with respect.

NO LAUGHING MATTER

Love is not arrogant or rude.

Years ago I was playing tennis on a public court in New Jersey. On the next court was a young couple. He was teaching her how to play. I couldn't help noticing that every time she made a mistake he wouldn't simply correct her but did it in such a way that made her look foolish. Of course, the more he made fun of her, the worse she got! Being pathologically unable to mind my own business, I wanted to rush over to the court and shout at the young woman, "If you're thinking of marrying this oaf—forget it! Don't do it! In fact, leave now!"

I didn't do it—the young man was built like Arnold Schwarzenegger and I am a card-carrying coward.

I often wondered if the young man on the tennis court was the groom who was the subject of one young woman's fears. In this case the woman in question wasn't the bride, but her best friend, who came to me when she had been asked to serve as maid of honor at the wedding.

"The trouble is," she said, "I don't think much of her fiancé. He has a way of speaking about her that at first sounds like a compliment or maybe a joke but inevitably reveals itself as a cleverly phrased insult. No subject, whether it's her weight or her family, is immune from his verbal gymnastics."

> Never marry a man who makes jokes at your expense.

The young woman agreed to stand by her friend, despite her fears. To her horror, when the wedding day finally arrived, the best man, who had been the groom's roommate at boarding school, rose to give this toast at the reception. In front of two hundred or so people he said:

"I would like to congratulate the groom on finally deciding to settle down with just one woman. I know it took a lot of self-restraint, but at the ripe old age of thirty-two, he's matured somewhat. Before I toast the bride and groom, I would like to ask all of the women the groom has dated to please come to the head table and return their keys to his apartment."

And with that, fourteen women approached the table, keys in hand. Joke or no joke, the bride was devastated.

The marriage lasted two years.

Learning Your Lessons

It's one thing to have standards. It's quite another to try to enforce them through rules. Try not to get caught up in dating rules, whether socially or self-imposed. If you find yourself relying on them to protect yourself, well, this may be a good time to examine those past relationships that have not lasted more than a few months. Ask and answer these questions honestly. You may find some valuable lessons here.

- Why did your previous relationships fall apart?

- Who instigated the breakups?

- Were the breakups amicable?

- Were you clear about what you wanted from the relationship?

- Were you intimate too soon?

- Do you talk about your ex-boyfriends with fondness—or animosity?

- Do you tend to pick the same "type" of guy over and over?

- Is there a common denominator to these past relationships?

Pride Goes Before the Fall

Never marry a pompous man. He'll look down on others—and perhaps you. A humble man is a much better bet, especially one who can laugh at himself and especially when his own self-importance has been punctured.

Years ago, I celebrated Mass in a New Jersey parish and afterward was standing in the vestibule of the church, farewelling the worshippers, when a teenage girl came gushing up to me, crying out, "Father, Father, what's your name?"

I thought to myself, *I really got through to this child.* Fishing for a compliment, I said, "Why do you want to know my name?"

She said, "My mother won't believe I've been to church unless I can tell her the name of the priest who said Mass."

Squelch!

THE TWIN ARTS OF TRUTH AND FORGIVENESS

In order for a relationship to work, a couple needs to practice the twin arts of truth and forgiveness. Yes, *arts.*

It would be a miracle if, even during courtship,

there was no conflict, no fighting. Even when you are very much in love, there will be disagreements. This may be one of the hardest lessons to learn, but it's one of the most important. A lively exchange of opinions can help a marriage flourish, as long as it's built on a foundation of love and respect.

If your boyfriend or husband is speaking the truth, it is your responsibility to listen without judgment, to hear what is really being said, and—even if you don't like what is being said—to respond frankly, with respect and kindness. Truth is that proverbial two-way street.

SPEAK THE TRUTH IN LOVE

A lot of husbands and wives I counsel may be courteous to one another, but they haven't had a frank conversation in years. More often than not, it's the man who's neglected to share his feelings, although sometimes quite the opposite is true; a husband and wife may be frank—brutally frank—but not courteous or respectful of one another.

Take my mother on marriage and frankness.

"If I had practiced perfect frankness with that

**LOVE IS NOT
ENVIOUS**

Lesson Six

Even an uncomfortable truth can be expressed with kindness and respect.

man"—pointing to my father on his third beer—"our marriage wouldn't have lasted six months!"

"But Mum," I said to her, a devout Catholic, "St. Paul tells us, 'In all your dealings with one another—in marriage, friendship, and community—speak the truth to one another in love, so that you may grow up.'"

"Paul was wrong," said Mum.

And that was the end of that.

My mother had very definite views on marriage, and men too. I remember when I was a boy hearing my mother chat with our next-door neighbor, whom I'll call Mrs. Brown, during one of their marathon conversations over the back fence.

Mrs. Brown had two daughters. This was a convenient arrangement for all concerned; that is, one daughter was my age, the other my brother's. The two girls taught us males how to behave in a civilized manner at parties, and we brothers taught them how to play Rugby and cricket!

Mrs. Brown had to cope with only one male—her husband. My mother, on the other hand, had to contend with three.

Mrs. Brown once asked my mother, in the presence of my father, my brother, and me, "You live with three men, seemingly harmoniously. And you've done it for so long. . . . What's the secret?"

My mother's answer to the question was delivered with awesome and comical arrogance. "You simply have to operate on the assumption that no man"—gazing at each of us in turn—"matures after the age of eleven!"

Is it any wonder I became a priest?!

LOVE IS NOT
ENVIOUS

Lesson Seven

Speak the truth in love.

....

The Seven Lessons of
*Love Is Not Envious or Boastful
or Arrogant or Rude*

1. Envy and jealousy are dangerous ingredients in any relationship.

2. Feelings aren't right or wrong in themselves. It's what you do with them that counts.

3. Sometimes love needs to say "I'm sorry."

4. Beware of cultivating a relationship with a man who is not humble.

5. Rules are good servants but bad masters.

6. Even an uncomfortable truth can be expressed with kindness and respect.

7. Speak the truth in love.

....

FIVE

Love Does Not Insist
on Its Own Way

COURTESY COUNTS

Think of how you go about your day, the people you come across, the things you do. How much better is that day when people are courteous to one another? A simple *please* and *thank you* or a smile from a stranger can make a big difference. Likewise, a rude remark, a door carelessly let go in your face— what thoughtlessness! How it can sting.

Manners are important. Period. I'm not talking about etiquette or the social graces. I'm talking about being aware of the people around you, of treating them with respect and dignity. That's what it really comes down to.

> *Manners are a sensitive awareness of the feelings of others. If you have that awareness, you have good manners, no manner what fork you use.*
>
> —EMILY POST

We're all busy. We're all trying to do too much in too little time. But little things really do mean a lot—the *pleases*, the *thank yous*, the simple words and acts of courtesy. Never underestimate the importance of civility in each day. And never underestimate the importance of civility in each relationship.

THANK YOU— TWO VERY POWERFUL WORDS

Three nights after the tragic events of September 11, a man and his wife were at a restaurant overlooking the smoldering skyline of lower Manhattan. Though it hardly seemed like a night to celebrate, someone

LOVE DOES NOT
INSIST ON ITS
OWN WAY

Lesson One

Great matters can turn on
simple courtesy.

close to them was marking a significant birthday.
Midway through their meal, a group of men in uni-
form arrived.

The man turned to his wife and said, "I wonder if
these guys are coming from the site. I'm going to go
find out."

He approached the captain, who confirmed that
this was their first hot meal in three days.

"May I have the honor of buying you dinner?"

The captain replied, "But there are twenty-three
of us."

"I may never have another chance to thank you."

And with that, he signaled the waiter. Clink-
ing his glass to silence the restaurant, the man

announced, "These men from all over the country have just spent the past seventy-two hours at the World Trade Center rescue operation. Will you all join me in recognizing their heroism?"

All present erupted into an emotional ovation.

The wife of the man who had made the toast looked at him with tears in her eyes. "My dear husband," she said. "You have just spent two car payments on this dinner. I have never loved you more than I do at this moment. I have never been more grateful to have you as my partner."

We would all do well to emulate the utter selflessness of these people, each of whom, in their own way, knew the value of the words *thank you*.

LOVE DOES NOT
INSIST ON ITS
OWN WAY

Lesson Two

A good marriage contains equal parts respect and gratitude.

Wedding **Bells** **OR** WARNING **Bells?**

I KNEW HE WASN'T THE GUY FOR ME WHEN . . .

◁ He was rude to the waitress.

◁ He called me Laurie (my name is Louise).

◁ He showed up for our second date wearing a NO FAT CHICKS T-shirt.

◁ He left our date early to visit an ex who was "having a hard time."

◁ He never once said *please* or *thank you*.

◁ He flew off the handle at the guy in front of us at the movies. (A simple *shhh* would have worked just as well!)

◁ He told a racist joke.

JOSIE'S STORY

Josie and Leo had been together since high school. Now in their early twenties, they were planning their wedding. Josie would joke that they would tell their children that he had been the high school quarterback and she a cheerleader. In fact, nothing was further from the truth. She was a science geek and he was a math nerd. Josie was a pretty girl. She was also smart and kind. Leo may have been the studious type, but he was also "quite the hunk," as Josie put it. Still, in that unfortunate caste system that is high school, they were outsiders—never sitting at the cool table in the cafeteria, never invited to the best parties. Josie and Leo didn't seem to mind. In fact, they attributed their outsider status to bringing them together in the first place.

"High school wasn't the happiest time for us . . . not until we met anyway," Josie explained when they came to see me for premarital counseling. "I always felt there was such surface stuff going on: who was wearing the latest jeans, who had the cool sunglasses, who had the shiniest hair. I like to look good too, but come on. I mean, they're just jeans! It's just hair!" Josie laughed as she tossed her hair in her best super-model impersonation.

Leo continued, "That kind of stuff, that's for losers. Those other people . . . the jocks and the queen bees or whatever they're calling themselves this week . . . they can have it. It's all so random, so subject to whim."

I was uncomfortable with Leo's remark about "losers" and "other people," and wondered whether he was trying to protect himself or if he really felt the "them and us" attitude that this, and other of his comments, conveyed. Still, he was talking about high school, a time that can bring up all sorts of feelings. I decided to focus on the positives. Leo and Josie were clear in their devotion to one another and they seemed to have a strong sense of who they were— both as individuals and as a couple. I liked the way the two of them bantered back and forth and the way each seemed to respect the other's views. They were lively and affectionate and fun. They had opinions and weren't afraid to share them—with each other or with me.

Can your partner hold opinions without insisting that you share them?

At this point in the conversation Josie interrupted with a smile. "Oh, oh, Father Pat, watch out! Here comes the math speech."

"You laugh," he said. "But you know *exactly* what I'm talking about. Math teaches you to think objectively. It's logical and reliable and it's incredibly powerful."

"Powerful?" I asked.

"Yes, Father Pat, *powerful*. Understanding math can release certain neurotransmitters in the brain. They provide a euphoric sensation that prompts a feeling of well-being and power. There's a real sense of authority associated with math. Trust me on this one. It's like the mysteries of the universe are being revealed to you because of your mental capacities. It's like religion!"

At that point I wondered if I should scrap next Sunday's sermon and give the congregation some fractions to work through instead.

"Math is absolute," Leo concluded. "It's not

subjective in the way other disciplines are. In a math problem there's only one correct answer. There are no *maybes* in math."

Better bend than break.

—SCOTTISH PROVERB

I couldn't help myself. "That *may be*," I said, "but there are many *maybes* in life. I don't think you can insist on the same mathematical principles in day-to-day living, and especially not in a relationship. There just isn't the same certainty."

"Yes but—"

"No buts," I said. "You two are obviously very much in love and I'm happy for you. But you need to realize that love isn't an absolute in the same way math is. Love does not insist on its own way," I reminded him.

I knew when I had a captive audience, so I continued.

"Leo, you obviously feel very strongly about the authority in math. But what about the authority in your relationship? Is that something that you're will-ing to share?"

The young couple was quiet for a moment.

Josie turned to him, a little unsure. "Sweetie? I'd say yes. How about you?"

Leo smiled and kissed her on the cheek. "A big affirmative," he said.

This lovely young couple came to see me several times after that first meeting. They had taken to heart my impromptu sermon on the danger of insisting on absolutes, and that opened up some great discussions on the subject of compromise and communication. They understood how important balance is to a healthy marriage, and that while they are two equal partners ("two components of the same equation" is how Leo put it), they won't be equal in every situation and every day. They talked openly about their expec-tations in marriage, about each other's strengths and weaknesses. When it came time for them to say "I do," they did so with confidence.

Has the marriage worked out?

Well, they've been married now for eight happy years. You do the math.

LOVE DOES NOT
INSIST ON ITS
OWN WAY

Lesson Three

You must be willing to share the authority in your relationship.

COMMON GROUND

Think back to when you met your fiancé. What was it that attracted you to him? I'm guessing there was some chemistry involved. And once you admitted your attraction to each other, well, I'm guessing that you found many things in common, too. "We both studied Spanish poetry!" I'll hear people say. "We both love General Tso's chicken." "We both have a birthmark in the shape of Texas! What are the odds?"

Sometimes we're a little facile in the way we look for connections. The online dating sites, for example, ask members to list their favorite _____ [fill in the blank], as if that were any indication of true compatibility. I've heard of some very random questions indeed:

- *What is your favorite color?*
- *What is written on your favorite T-shirt?*
- *What is your favorite movie?*
- *What animal do you most identify with?*

If he wears a blue T-shirt from his favorite brewery while watching *Julie & Julia* and wishing he was a koala bear—well, what on earth does that tell you about him? It doesn't amount to anything.

> *Whoever said that*
> *all men were created equal*
> *never tried online dating.*

A person's favorite movie may tell you something about his personality, but it won't divulge his character. Still, the familiar is thrilling when you first fall in love. You look for commonalities, things you can share. Of course you know that you will have differences, and in the beginning even these seem exciting. The woman who's a planner at heart will be taken by her boy-friend's spontaneity. The woman who has a wild side may enjoy her boyfriend's more cautious nature.

But as the wedding draws near it's important to look past these superficial qualities to see what's really important. Character counts in a marriage much more than these commonalities do. Does it really matter if his favorite color is blue or if you love the same music? Listen to your instincts and try to think not just of the man, but of the marriage you will make together. Many things aren't worth worrying about, but big deal differences often lead to big problems. Pay attention to them now before you walk down that aisle.

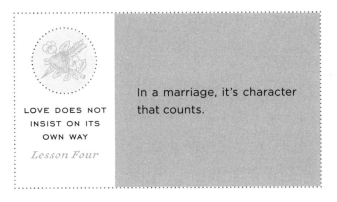

LOVE DOES NOT
INSIST ON ITS
OWN WAY

Lesson Four

In a marriage, it's character that counts.

Wedding **Bells** WARNING **Bells?**

+ You're a saver; he's a spendthrift. Your attitude toward finances is important. How you each deal with money even more so. I've seen many a love match dissolve over financial difficulties. Talk candidly to your partner about your expectations *before* you walk down the aisle.

+ You're an optimist; he's a pessimist. You say the glass is half-empty. He says the glass is half-full. Your differing viewpoints may bring a sense of balance to your relationship, but over time they could turn into a tug-of-war. Respect each other's viewpoints and you should be fine.

+ You want children; he doesn't. Don't marry him!

+ You enjoy a glass of wine; he drinks to excess. You may love a man with a drinking problem, but don't marry him. He may promise to get help for his alcohol abuse (or his abuse of any substance for that matter), but he's got to do so *before* the wedding. And not a week or two, or even a month or two. If he's really serious about your relationship, he'll make sure that he's sober for a full year before the wedding.

Dear Father Pat

Dear Father Pat: My boyfriend regularly sends birthday cards to his ex-girlfriends, but it makes me uncomfortable. What should I make of it? Signed: *Confused*

Dear Confused: You don't need me to tell you what to make of it—you've already told me! It makes you uncomfortable. This man is being disrespectful to your relationship and you know it. Get rid of him and join the ranks of his ex-girlfriends. Think of the birthday cards to come!

SEPARATE BUT EQUAL

Imagine a woman and a man making a visit to a sprawling antiques pavilion. There is a seemingly endless array of showcases and display cabinets of items from the last two centuries. She is drawn to some drawers full of vintage gloves; he is fascinated by a wall of 1940s movie posters. As they browse the store, each is content. If one comes across an object of particular interest, the first impulse is to call the other over to share in the moment of discovery. They pass hours in this manner, enjoying companionship free from any obligation to experience the outing in exactly the same way. Over dinner later, they will compare notes about the unusual things they saw, deepening their relationship.

> *The most beautiful discovery true friends make is that they can grow separately without growing apart.*
>
> —ELISABETH FOLEY

Does your boyfriend encourage you to pursue your own interests, even those with which he has no attraction or familiarity?

I've seen marriages work when the couple doesn't have the same interests across the board but tolerate or encourage the other's divergent interests. The engagement period is the time to sort through that. For example, one spouse-to-be might love skiing and might want to enjoy that sport every weekend and vacation day. But if his bookish wife isn't one for the slopes they'll have to come to a compromise, one that includes his likes and hers.

> *Love has nothing to do with what you are expecting to get—only with what you are expecting to give— which is everything.*
>
> —KATHARINE HEPBURN

One woman I know wondered how she might plan a life with her boyfriend, who loved watching ESPN with the volume turned up loud. "I hate the noise and the violence. I just don't see the point of it," she told me. "Father Pat, can you suggest a mutually satisfying compromise?"

"If you can," I said, "let him have a room to

himself, where he can watch his sports programs in noisy solitude. He'll get his sports and you'll get your peace."

Then there is a happily married couple I know in which the *wife* is the football fanatic. From September to January she is glued to the TV set, screaming her encouragement to her favorite team. Her husband, who has not the slightest interest in football, is vastly amused by this reversal of the traditional husband-wife roles and by his wife's devotion to the New York Giants. Moreover, he cooks Sunday dinner.

I'm glad when prospective spouses use the word *compromise.* In most human relationships compromise

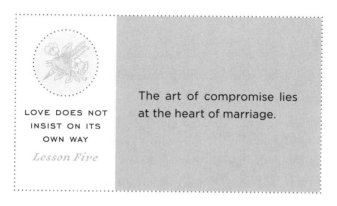

LOVE DOES NOT
INSIST ON ITS
OWN WAY

Lesson Five

The art of compromise lies
at the heart of marriage.

is the name of the game, for if every individual always insists on his views taking precedence, you'll have chaos, in the home, in married life, in the workplace, wherever.

OR FOREVER HOLD YOUR PEACE

There are times in your relationship when you'll have to speak up. If your partner refuses to support you or take your side in a conflict, you'll need to let him know you're upset. The problem will only persist if left unaddressed.

> Resentment in a relationship can grow like weeds in a garden. Tend to your relationship with respect and openness. Be honest with your partner about what's bothering you. Only then can you deal with what's wrong and move on.

That's what happened with one young couple. It was their first Christmas and the newlyweds were dealing with an all too common problem: choosing which family to spend the holidays with. The groom's family had hosted many consecutive gatherings while the couple had been engaged, so the bride was pleased to hear her husband suggest that they celebrate Christmas with her parents. Her beloved aunt was ill at the time and recuperating at her parents', so the change of venue—the change of heart, really—was very welcome.

The bride and her mother cooked all day, preparing for the arrival of the newly combined family, while a heavy snow fell outside. Once it was apparent that the Christmas flakes had become a blizzard, the phone rang. It was the groom's mother, expressing regret that they would not be able to attend. "We can't leave Grandma on her own," she said, "and you know that your father doesn't like to drive in weather like this." She proposed instead that the bride's family drive all the food back to their place.

The young husband was torn. He didn't want to disappoint his parents or his elderly grandmother. He was a much better driver than his father (this was a joke in the family), and felt no qualms about driving through the snow. Still, the task of packing up the food and getting everybody to his mother's house was not something he relished. He approached his bride with the problem, and asked if she would mind very much heading out to his family's house.

Now it was the young bride who was torn. She was faced with the impossible choice of spending her first Christmas as a married woman with her husband and his family, or staying by the side of her ailing aunt. In the end, she gave in, and they packed up the food and made a harrowing drive across icy roads. Her aunt spent Christmas alone.

> *Speaking up is a question of*
> *retaining your own dignity.*

Upset as she was, the newlywed bride had been reluctant to voice her concerns over what had happened. She didn't want her first Christmas as a wife to be surrounded by arguments, nor did she want to be put in the position of debating who was more important, her husband's grandmother or her aunt. It wasn't until the next fall, when planning for the upcoming holiday season commenced, that her resentment flew to the surface like a wild bird.

"I can't believe there's even an issue here!" she said. "Last Christmas was ruined . . . not by the snow, but by you and your mother. And your father! I don't know what to say about him. What kind of grown man can't drive a few miles through the snow? I've never heard of such a thing!"

Her husband was struck dumb at the fury in her feelings. She had seemed so willing at the time that he had no idea of the depth of her animosity over the event.

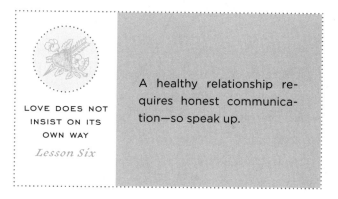

LOVE DOES NOT
INSIST ON ITS
OWN WAY

Lesson Six

A healthy relationship requires honest communication—so speak up.

"Honey," he said, "I had no idea how you felt. Why didn't you tell me at the time?"

Why indeed?

LOCATION, LOCATION, LOCATION

Recently a young woman asked me for help in her predicament.

"My boyfriend is in graduate school," she told me. "He has ambitions to get a government job. After spending a year apart, we got engaged. I relocated from our small hometown in the Midwest to be with him in Washington. He says maybe in six to eight years we can move back home.

"I've tried to make a good life for us here, but after almost a year, I know in my heart that I'm a small-town girl. I am very close to my family and friends, and miss them terribly. He, on the other hand, values work over family, and is not bothered by seeing his relatives infrequently. I know that marriage involves compromise, but I feel like I'm living his life and sacrificing my happiness for him. I want to spend the rest of my life with him, but I don't think I can spend the next five or more years living like this."

> Don't marry a man who is too selfish to do himself what he asks of you.

Remember: You can love someone dearly but be unable to have a happy marriage with him. I think that's the case in this relationship. Here is a man who values work over his family, who doesn't seem willing to make the compromises he's asking of his girlfriend. She is very close to her family and friends—he is not. She loves her small hometown—he talks vaguely about moving there in six or eight years. These are important issues they disagree on. While travel is much easier these days, the inconvenience and irregular visiting schedule won't suffice for this bride. She has to make a decision: family and friends and small town versus the beloved, who values work over family and prefers city life over the small town.

My view is they should split.

LOVE DOES NOT
INSIST ON ITS
OWN WAY

Lesson Seven

Make sure your partner is willing to make the sacrifices he is asking of you.

OUT OF CONTROL

"I have a friend," one woman told me, "whose fiancé is very charming but tries to control everything she does. He keeps track of where she is at all times. She even has to check in with him!"

This young woman's situation brought to mind the frightening lyrics to a number-one song by The Police titled "Every Breath You Take." Sung from the perspective of a menacing, controlling character, the refrain, "I'll be watching you," reveals the explosive combination of passion and violence of which such a person might be capable.

Is Your Relationship Guided by Mutual Respect?

Are your life decisions made in consultation with one another?

Do you feel restful and at ease when you are together rather than being under a strain?

Do you admire your boyfriend for what he is and for what he has accomplished in life?

Are you proud to be seen with him in public and by your friends and relatives?

Do you believe your love could weather the storms of financial distress, sickness, and serious misunderstanding?

Is your boyfriend always striving to put you in a favorable light when you are out among friends?

Sting himself had married an actress and wrote the song as the union was collapsing. In a 1993 interview he said, "I woke up in the middle of the night with that line in my head, sat down at the piano and had written it in half an hour. . . . It sounds like a comforting love song. I didn't realize at the time how sinister it is. I think I was thinking of Big Brother, surveillance and control."

> Never marry a man who tries to control you.

When I mentioned this song to the woman who had come to see me, she nodded her head vigorously. "Yes," she said. "That's exactly what it's like. Big Brother. Only there's nothing brotherly about it!"

I felt for the young woman before me and for her friend too. A controlling relationship is difficult for anybody to endure.

She continued, "My friend's fiancé is very bossy and quick to lose his temper. He tries to limit her contact with her friends—at least when he's not around—and he tells her what to wear. Sometimes he seems incredibly loving toward her, showering her with gifts, taking her to the theater, telling her how much he loves her and how he can't live without her."

"And the other times?" I asked.

"Well, he tries to keep her down. For example, he seems to have robbed her of her confidence. Recently she was going to apply for a new job but he told her not to bother, that she'd never get it."

"And?" I asked.

"She was so down on herself after his remarks that she didn't even send in her resume. Look," she continued, "I've watched enough Lifetime television to know that he might be abusive."

At that she caught herself. "Sorry, Father Pat. Bad joke. It's just that I'm worried about her and don't know how to approach the situation. I don't think he's hit her or anything like that, but this is not okay. What should I do?"

Respect is what we owe;
love what we give.

— PHILIP JAMES BAILEY

This is a terrible situation for anyone to be in, but I applaud this young woman for taking her friend's well-being seriously. I suggested that she pull her friend aside and speak candidly to her. She should confide her fears, and let her friend know that she's not alone.

"Tell her you notice that she doesn't seem to be relaxed around her fiancé," I said. "And let her know that you love and respect her. Offer her any and all help that you can—including a couch to sleep on if that's needed—and try to alleviate any feelings of shame or embarrassment she may be feeling. This is not her fault. But she may feel that it is. Above all, let her know that you are her friend and that you will be there for her—no matter what."

There are many reasons a woman will put up with a controlling relationship:

- *She may have a distorted sense of love.*
- *She may believe she has no choice.*
- *She may be lonely.*
- *She may not realize the extent to which her boyfriend is controlling the relationship.*
- *She may believe her boyfriend will change.*
- *She may be scared to leave.*

LOVE DOES NOT
INSIST ON ITS
OWN WAY

Lesson Eight

Marriage must be based on
mutual respect.

There is no reason for a woman to put up with a controlling or abusive relationship, whether that abuse is
physical or emotional. Even if this man is not abusive,
his suitability as a marriage partner is nil if he tries to
control everything his fiancée does and everyone she
sees. Marriage should be based on mutual respect and
love. This woman should not marry this man!

. . . .

The Eight Lessons of *Love Does Not Insist on Its Own Way*

1. Great matters can turn on simple courtesy.

2. A good marriage contains equal parts respect and gratitude.

3. You must be willing to share the authority in your relationship.

4. In a marriage, it's character that counts.

5. The art of compromise lies at the heart of marriage.

6. A healthy relationship requires honest communication—so speak up.

7. Make sure your partner is willing to make the sacrifices he is asking of you.

8. Marriage must be based on mutual respect.

. . . .

SIX

Love Is Not Irritable
or Resentful

MARRIAGE—A PERSONAL CHOICE

There is no choice more personal than the decision to enter into marriage. Yet, as preparations for the wedding ceremony begin, it can be all too tempting for couples to focus on the external and material rather than the internal and emotional or spiritual.

Most couples come to see me with an open mind and an open heart, genuinely interested in exploring their relationship before they say "I do." Sometimes, however (and thankfully this doesn't happen that often), I have the feeling that I'm just another item on their to-do list, something to attend to after the invitations and the flowers.

And then there are the couples who are interested not just in their relationship, but in the relationships of everyone around them.

One engaged woman told me, "Attending our pre-marriage counseling sessions, my fiancé and I couldn't help but observe the other couples in our class. We were troubled to notice a disturbing trend, that half of them seemed to be getting married because they were *supposed to*: according to age, pressure from family members, whatever. When asked to express their goals, these couples could have been speaking in one voice. They talked about setting up identical

LOVE IS NOT
IRRITABLE OR
RESENTFUL

Lesson One

Settling down is not the same as settling.

life plans—buying a house, having children, saving for retirement."

The woman's observations of her classmates set her to worrying.

"My fiancé and I . . ." She hesitated. "We're adventurous people. We want a less conventional life. We want to travel. We want to explore. We want to take nothing for granted. This whole white picket fence thing . . . sheesh. It gives me hives!"

She took a moment to compose herself.

"Father Pat, are we wrong to have such an adverse reaction to other couples' plans for 'settling down'?"

"It's not a matter of right or wrong," I told her. "Try not to be so harsh. Your companions are opting for a philosophy of marriage that includes settling down. That's fine for them if that's what they want."

"Really, Father Pat?" she asked.

"Really," I said. "You think that *settling down*, as these people are doing, is the same thing as *settling*, and that's just not the case. 'There's no accounting for taste,' and this goes double for married lifestyles. I urge you not to judge the other couples. They have chosen their way. You have chosen yours."

Believe nothing just because a so-called wise person said it. Believe nothing just because a belief is generally held. Believe nothing just because it is said in ancient books. Believe nothing just because it is said to be of divine origin. Believe nothing just because someone else believes it. Believe only what you yourself test and judge to be true.

—BUDDHA

I advised this young woman to ask herself why she was so concerned with the motives of her companions. Was she perhaps focusing on other relationships to take her mind off her own? I've seen it happen. Women and men alike will focus on all manner of externals to avoid thinking of the big step they are about to take in their own lives. After talking more with this young woman and—more importantly— listening, I believed this wasn't true in her case. It was as she had said: She had such a solid idea of what her marriage should be that she thought of anything else as something *less*.

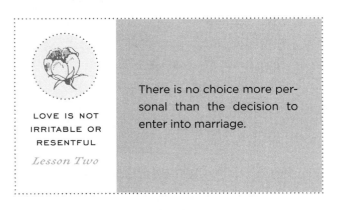

LOVE IS NOT
IRRITABLE OR
RESENTFUL

Lesson Two

There is no choice more personal than the decision to enter into marriage.

GREAT EXPECTATIONS

It's important to be aware of your expectations of marriage before you enter into it. Even if it's difficult to admit certain realities to yourself, do so. Imagine your wedding day as the first of many that will follow in married life. Develop your sense of self-awareness and observation so that you and your intended can protect your values and principles from a too-great influence by others.

Write down your anticipations so that you'll be sure to recognize them if the pertinent circumstances unfold before you:

- *My expectations*
- *My future partner's expectations*
- *My parents' expectations*
- *My future in-laws' expectations*
- *My disappointment so far*
- *My cherished dream*

Your marriage is not your parents' marriage, nor is it the marriage of your friends, coworkers, or neighbors. Comparing your own intimate relationship to one involving outside parties is not only dangerous, but potentially disastrous.

A TOUGH ACT TO FOLLOW

Some people can get overly attached to the example of their parents' marriage.

"Many friends who knew my parents," one man told me, "have told me that one reason I'm not

LOVE IS NOT
IRRITABLE OR
RESENTFUL

Lesson Three

Comparing your relationship to others will only sow the seeds of resentment.

married is that my parents' marriage was a tough act to follow and that my expectations are too high. How can I start to think of my own potential marriage more independently?"

"You might begin," I suggested, "by taking a good look at your parents' *perfect* marriage. What are some of the behaviors that stand out? Did each have a tolerance for the other's contrary views? My own father, for example, used to love to watch my brother and me play Rugby. My mother was convinced Rugby was a barbaric endeavor (she was probably right) and would not walk across the road to watch my brother and me in action. Yet, to her credit, she never tried to force her views about Rugby and boxing on my father or us boys.

"Second," I continued. "Ask your parents what they thought they did right. The answers to these questions may furnish you with good foundations for your own married life. I say may, because your situation in marriage may be entirely different from theirs."

And then there is the opposite problem.

Consider the story of the young man who felt as if his life ended at nine, when his parents divorced. Even at twenty-seven, all of his cultural references, hobbies, and behaviors centered around the "golden era" of his boyhood. In every other way, from his job to his personal life, he behaved in an adult fashion. Yet though he longed to ask women out on dates, he had never had the courage to do so. Finally succumbing to peer pressure, he began dating a woman, who turned out to like him very much. In spite of his romantic feelings toward her, he never felt secure enough to pursue the relationship beyond the most superficial level. Over the next several years, he dated a few different women with the same result. He never married and now lives alone with his regrets.

Just as there are many right reasons to enter into marriage, there are many wrong reasons to avoid marriage. That decision, if made according to negative

LOVE IS NOT
IRRITABLE OR
RESENTFUL

Lesson Four

When considering marriage it's important to ask "What will work for me?"

examples, would be a serious mistake. If you do meet someone who is right for you, opt for a lengthy engagement, so you can not only get to know one another but yourself as well to be sure you are ready to marry.

It is always important to ask "What will work for me?" You are you. Your parents are other people entirely. What worked for them may not work for you. Have the courage to break free from their example—positive though it may be. It's important to realize that there are multiple sources of wisdom out there about whom to marry—and whom not to marry—and your task is to delve into them, leaving your parents' marriage as a completely separate entity.

SUSAN'S STORY

Susan and Richard had grown up in the same small town. Her father owned a shoe factory and was the biggest employer for miles around. Richard's mother and father both worked in the factory, as did Richard during his high school summers. Susan was something of a golden girl. A cheerleader and class president, she had all the boys drooling after her, Richard included. He couldn't believe it when she said she'd go out with him. He was nervous about the date and spent a week planning what they would do. Where usually he would take a girl to the local burger joint for a bite to eat, he took Susan to a fancy French restaurant and blew two weeks' wages from his part-time job. Susan was sweet and seemed to enjoy the date, but Richard was nervous and felt he didn't make a good impression.

Apparently he did, because they dated on and off after that. Nothing serious—a movie here, a basketball game there. Susan seemed to like Richard well enough. She thought he was smart and funny; she cracked up whenever he'd imitate Mr. Desmond, their math teacher. Susan knew that Richard didn't have as much money as the boys she usually dated, but she didn't mind. What she did mind, however, was the way he doted on her, the way he catered to her every whim. He always let her pick the movie, he never let her pay for anything, and if she was in a bad mood *he* would be the one to apologize. And as for the presents! Susan only had to mention something—anything—whether it be a song she heard on the radio or a necklace at a local boutique, and Richard would buy it for her. At first Susan thought it was charming. She even referred to him as *My Prince Charming*. But after a while it started to get on her nerves. Susan felt her dad already treated her as his little princess. She didn't want her boyfriend doing the same, so they stopped seeing each other.

Nobody can make you feel inferior without your permission.

—ELEANOR ROOSEVELT

College came, and they went their separate ways. Susan went to Brown, a third-generation legacy.

Richard went to a state school and became the first college graduate in his family. After graduation, unbeknownst to one another, they each moved to Chicago. Susan went to law school, and then became an associate in a midsized corporate law firm, and Richard found a promising job with a tech start-up. Susan found the position more of a challenge than she had anticipated, and despite her four years at college and three years in law school, she felt out of sync with her new colleagues. She had always prided herself on the fact that she hadn't defined herself by her money and status, but now that she was in the big city with people who had a lot more money and social standing than she did, she felt a little out of her league.

Richard, for his part, was doing very well. He enjoyed his new job and the thrill of being in on the ground floor of something. He was respected by his colleagues and well liked, and because of that, found himself becoming more confident—proud, even.

One day, a couple of years after moving to Chicago, Richard and Susan bumped into each other at a party. They were delighted to see each other and wasted no time in catching up. Susan found a cozy corner where they could chat while Richard made a beeline for the bar. They discussed their respective college experiences. Susan talked about life at Brown, about the professors she loved and the ones she didn't. Richard talked about his school and had Susan laughing at his roommate horror stories. They talked about old times, and Richard ended the evening with an encore performance of Mr. Desmond, their old math teacher.

Within a few weeks, Richard had worked up the nerve to ask his one-time girlfriend for a date. She gladly accepted.

This young couple had both changed since their high school days, but it was hard for them to see that in the other. Ironically, while Susan may have become more impressed with status and money than she had ever been, she clung to Richard because he knew her as the golden girl she once was. With Richard she felt important, more like the Queen Bee than the wannabe. Richard had changed since high school and had really grown; unfortunately he seemed to regress somewhat around Susan, whom he saw as a symbol of everything he had once wanted out of life. They dated seriously for about seven months, after which time Richard asked Susan to marry him. Much to his delight, she accepted his proposal.

> *A loving person tries to live by the Golden Rule: Do unto others as you would have them do unto you.*

Her parents threw them a lavish wedding, and from the moment they moved into their new home, he treated her as the treasure he felt she was. He never stopped praising her to his friends at work, never stopped deferring to her in their home or when they were out with friends. He would check in with her before he made any decision, no matter how small. He even called her "princess!" In return Susan responded by ordering him around like her employee or even a servant.

"The phone's ringing," she would say. "Hadn't you better answer it?"

"Didn't you pick up the dry cleaning today? I wanted to wear my blue dress out tonight."

"Oh, why did you buy that Merlot? You know I don't like that vineyard."

It went from bad to worse. Richard could see that their marriage was headed down the wrong road, and he accepted his part in it, too. He tried to talk to Susan about it, to try to get her to understand that he was feeling resentful about being pushed around and that the marriage wasn't working. Susan wouldn't hear of it.

"You can't change the rules in the middle of the game," she said. "This is who I am. This is who you are. This is what our marriage is. Accept it."

But Richard couldn't accept it. He realized that he had entered into marriage not as an adult, but as a besotted high school student who was so taken with status and social standing that he entered into a marriage without love or respect. He had had enough.

LOVE IS NOT IRRITABLE OR RESENTFUL

Lesson Five

Steer clear of someone whose life you can run, who never makes demands counter to yours.

R. E. S. P. E. C. T.—
Find Out What It Means to Me

Aretha Franklin said it best. We all want a little respect. Nowhere is that more true than in a marriage, which must be based on the mutual respect husband and wife must have for one another.

Seeing my faults and loving me anyway—that's respect.—Cheryl C.

To me, respect means asking my opinion. —Kate M.

The day my boyfriend said, "I think you're wrong, but I support you anyway," I knew that he respected me.—Alicia R.

When I overheard my boyfriend telling his friends what a good job I did navigating a difficult situation at the office, I knew he respected not just my work, but me too.—Leslie K.

Listening! That's respect.—Mary O.

My husband loves our similarities. But he respects our differences.—Monica M.

Finally one night after one demand too many, Richard told her to pick up her own dry cleaning, to hire a maid, and to answer the phone herself. He was no longer her "domestic."

"I love you, Susan. There isn't anything I wouldn't do for you, but the key word here is *anything*. I've been doing *everything* for you and it's just not working."

"I knew I shouldn't have married a loser like you," Susan said. "You have a stupid job, stupid friends, and I find nothing attractive about you."

Doormat no more, he finally took charge and left.

THE BREAKFAST CLUB

Love is not irritable or resentful. And love is not selfish.

In the courtship phase the selfish person is easily recognized. He never thinks of putting your needs ahead of his. He is concerned with his desires and they will *always* take precedence over yours. That's why it's very important that you know what you want.

Sure, the selfish man may do things that seem to be giving. He may tell you how lovely you look.

He may hold the door open for you and pick up the check at dinner. That's all fine and good. These are accepted gestures—it's all part of the dating game. The selfish person constantly seeks his own advantage. He puts his own welfare ahead of anything else.

> Ask yourself this: Does your boyfriend try to pressure you into doing things that you don't want to do? Is he reluctant to take no for an answer?

A young woman I know told me about a man she had just met. Gretchen and John had communicated through an online dating site for a few weeks prior to their meeting. When she saw him at the bar she breathed a sigh of relief. *Finally*, she thought, *a guy who lives up to his picture.*

John was nice. Good-looking, successful, an up-and-coming associate in a big corporate law firm, he was what her mother would call "a catch." Gretchen knew enough to make their first meeting brief. She'd made the mistake before of arranging a dinner date with a guy she wanted to ditch before the appetizers came.

"I mean, really, Father Pat," she had asked me, "why would I be interested in his accordion lessons?"

This time, however, all went swimmingly. The designated hour (that's what Gretchen decided was a fair amount of time to give to a guy on a first date) flew by, and John asked Gretchen if she was free for dinner. "So what if I was breaking my first-date rule," she said with a smile. "Rules *are* made to be broken."

John was a gentleman. He took her to a lovely restaurant and the evening flew by in an exchange of stories and flirtations. He picked up the check without hesitation and shook his head at Gretchen's offer to help with the bill. They lingered over Irish coffees while the waitstaff cleaned up around them. All in all, a picture-perfect evening—until, that is, he started pressuring her to spend the night with him.

Never marry a selfish man.

Gretchen had been attracted to John the moment she met him, and it was obvious that the feeling was mutual. Still, while they had had been flirting with each other all evening, there was no question of her spending the night with him. Another first-date rule.

"Oh, c'mon, Gretchen honey," he said as he leaned in closer, "come home with me. I make a great breakfast."

Gretchen smiled. The breakfast line wasn't new, but it was cute. He followed it up with another attempt, one she hadn't heard: "Think of all the women on the *Titanic* who wished they had eaten dessert!"

"Oh brother," Gretchen told him, "you need to get some new material." Still, she liked John and was flattered. This wasn't the first time she'd had that request and it was unlikely to be the last.

"I'm not a nun," she told me. "I considered it for a moment. But only for a moment." She had no intention of going home with him, but his come-on didn't really bother her. Until, that is, he tried to seal the deal.

"What are you waiting for?" he asked. "Life is short and you *are* almost thirty."

Gretchen felt all the air leave her lungs. She was devastated. John's asking her to sleep with him on a first date didn't impress her, but it wasn't a deal breaker either. *This*, on the other hand, was. Gretchen believed that in those few words John told her what he really thought about his outlook on life and women, too. His get-it-while-you-can attitude was very much at odds with her way of thinking. Gretchen wasn't naïve, she didn't imagine that every date would turn into some fairy-tale happily ever after, but she knew what she wanted: someone kind and loving, someone who would share not just her desires, but her goals and beliefs too. She wanted someone who might be in it for the long haul, not just for the night. Strike one.

As for his you-are-almost-thirty crack, well, that didn't impress Gretchen in the least. "I'm not a carton of milk," she told me. "And I don't have an expiration date." Strike two.

LOVE IS NOT
IRRITABLE OR
RESENTFUL

Lesson Six

If you know what you want it's much easier to walk away from what you don't want.

Dear Father Pat

Dear Father Pat: I've heard people say that a woman should never marry a man who is less intelligent than she is. Do you agree? Signed: *Smart and Single*

Dear Smart: The jury is still out on that one, as far as I'm concerned. If you're significantly smarter or better educated than your husband you may find yourself frustrated at times. But know that there are many forms of intelligence—emotional intelligence, mathematical intelligence, musical intelligence, spiritual intelligence. Your husband will have many strengths and weaknesses, as will you. Respect them and you'll be fine.

Gretchen didn't wait for strike three. She grabbed her coat and made for a hasty exit, but not before giving him a piece of her mind. "You know, John," she said, "for a lawyer you make a lousy closing argument."

Take some time to ask yourself what you're looking

for in a mate. You don't have to be thinking *husband material* at the first-date stage. Just consider what it is about that first date that will get you to a second—and possibly commitment. And know what you want.

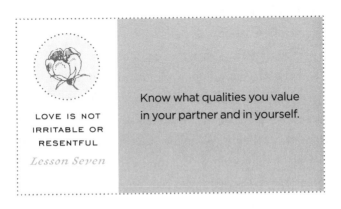

LOVE IS NOT
IRRITABLE OR
RESENTFUL

Lesson Seven

Know what qualities you value
in your partner and in yourself.

MR. WRITE

"When I was young," a woman once told me, "we had a lesson in our youth group about marriage. We were asked to write down the qualities we wanted in a husband, which I did. Then we were told to do our best to be that same person. Would you advocate this exercise as a preparation for marriage?"

I would. Not only as a preparation for marriage, but as an ongoing measure of how your marriage is changing over time. And it will! I would hope that you will keep checking your list—first, in class; again, as you begin to be serious about someone; and, again, frequently, after you marry.

See how he checks out.

The criteria you wrote as a young woman will likely change as you grow older. For example, in your first list, you might include good looks or sexy as desirable qualities in a husband. Later on you might rate those qualities as less important than a good sense of humor, kindness, or intelligence. This is a great exercise to help you focus on what you value not just in your partner, but in yourself.

....

The Seven Lessons of
Love Is Not Irritable or Resentful

1. Settling down is not the same as settling.

2. There is no choice more personal than the decision to enter into marriage.

3. Comparing your relationship to others will only sow the seeds of resentment.

4. When considering marriage it's important to ask "What will work for me?"

5. Steer clear of someone whose life you can run, who never makes demands counter to yours.

6. If you know what you want it's much easier to walk away from what you don't want.

7. Know what qualities you value in your partner and in yourself.

....

SEVEN

Love Does Not Rejoice in Wrongdoing, But Rejoices in the Truth

What greater thing is there
for two human souls
than to feel that
they are joined for life—
to strengthen each other in all labor,
to rest on each other in all sorrow,
to minister to each other in all pain,
to be one with each other in silent,
unspeakable memories at the moment
of the last parting.

—GEORGE ELIOT, *ADAM BEDE*

KEEPING SCORE

When I give sermons at weddings I like to quote Father Bill Bausch, who says that spouses have to be bad mathematicians, that is to say, they will not keep score about things done or not done. I've heard couples bicker back and forth over the smallest, most insignificant things: "You said you were going to take out the trash." "Your mother is coming over again?" "I can't believe you forgot you were supposed to pick me up." "You said you were going to do _____ [fill in the blank] last Tuesday and you never did." That bean-counter approach often adds up to an equation that can only be solved in divorce court.

It's important for couples to know how to resolve their differences because these differences will add up over time and, like water washing away rocks, will erode their marriage.

Most people want to have a loving, healthy, and peaceful marriage. In fact, young couples often ask me, "How do we achieve peace in a marriage, especially when that quality seems so absent from the world today?"

Peace in marriage is represented as concord and

harmony, and it results in a balanced union between two people. It doesn't mean that you won't have dissension or disagreements. You will have disagreements in your marriage. You will have arguments. Face up to that. And don't, as some people have done, go along with your spouse just to *keep the peace*. Peace is something that should be achieved by both persons in a marriage, not kept by one.

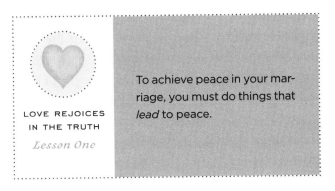

LOVE REJOICES
IN THE TRUTH

Lesson One

To achieve peace in your marriage, you must do things that *lead* to peace.

So, how do you achieve peace in marriage?

By doing habitually the things that lead to peace. That is to say, engage in open and honest communication with your mate. Practice the art of forgiveness. Speak the truth in love. Be generous toward your partner, and know that peace and love go hand in hand.

THE GIFT OF INSIGHT

I know that I've impressed upon you how important it is to enter into marriage with your eyes wide open. At the risk of sounding like an infomercial . . . *But wait! There's more!*

There is sight in its most physical sense, the kind that brings about the communication between our eyes and our brain. We depend on the gift of sight (and truly, it is a gift) not just to help us make our way in the world, but to understand all that is in it. "Seeing is believing," we say. And "I see what you mean." Or even, "I just can't see it." No doubt about it, we rely on our sight in a great many ways.

> *Regret is insight*
> *that comes a day too late.*
>
> —UNKNOWN

LOVE REJOICES
IN THE TRUTH
Lesson Two

Insight is a valuable commodity for daily life and a necessity for marriage.

And yet, there's another type of sight that is equally if not more important, and that's the enhancement of sight we call *insight*. Insight is the act of seeing not only the visual, but the verbal and emotional too. This type of seeing—which comes about partly by experience, partly by intuition—is crucial in grasping the true nature of things. Insight, which we can think of as sight from within, gives us a feeling of understanding, a sense that we "get" a situation for what it really is. Because the truth of life is that just as much as you have to be willing not to engage in wrongdoings in all your relationships, you still have to know how to protect yourself against them. And the best way you can do that is to trust your instincts and develop your insight.

CAROL'S STORY

Carol and Victor became engaged after a short court-ship. They were in their late twenties. This was a first marriage for both of them. Victor had, however, been engaged once before, but the relationship broke up be-fore the wedding took place. He never really discussed his previous engagement with Carol (she didn't even know who had broken up with whom), although he made a point of telling her he was completely over his ex. "I want to move on," he said. "Let's tie the knot."

A date was set and a hall was rented. Victor didn't seem to be very interested in the wedding details, so Carol took over the project. "You know, honey," he said, "I hope this doesn't sound awful, but I went through all this stuff with Leslie and I just don't think I have it in me to do it all again."

Carol jumped in like the good sport she was. "I'm my own wedding planner!" she joked to friends. She was a little concerned about his lack of involvement, and even wondered if it meant that he wasn't as keen on the wedding as he had first led her to believe, but she put her fears aside and busied herself with the preparations. "This really is a task best left up to the bride-to-be," she reasoned. "Men don't like to concern themselves with such things. If they did, wouldn't there be a magazine called *Modern Groom?*"

> Never marry a man you have to constantly make excuses for.

The couple had talked about buying a house to move into right after the wedding. He had even talked about carrying her over the threshold. However, whenever Carol asked him specific questions about their new home, such as "What neighborhood should we choose?" and "What would you prefer—an old house or a new construction?" Victor gave her vague answers. When pressed he backpedaled with "You know, interest rates are really volatile right now. I think we should wait."

So she waited.

As the wedding day approached, Victor became unusually busy at work. Nights and weekends he could be found at his desk behind a mound of paperwork. One evening he announced, "I need to postpone the wedding. The timing is going to conflict with a deadline at the office. I've already contacted the minister."

To the astonishment of her friends and family, Carol believed him.

The engagement went on for another year. Thinking that a simple wedding would be best at this point, Carol scaled back the reception plans from a dinner dance to a small cocktail party. When the revised date came near, Victor began a schedule of extended work trips. Due to his busy calendar, they cut down on their dates.

She thought it was an encouraging sign when Victor cancelled one of his business trips so that they could spend some time together. They dined against the backdrop of a glimmering cityscape, and that's when Victor dropped his bombshell.

"It's over," he said. "Leslie and I have patched it up. I'm going to marry her."

The desire to make a relationship work must come from two people. If it's one-sided, well, I think it's safe to say that the relationship itself is suffering.

Every happily married couple agrees that you have to work hard to keep the ship that is matrimony afloat—all this because both parties to the marriage are imperfect human beings whose faults and failings threaten to sink the boat. If you have to make excuses for your partner, well, determine why you must. If the situations that call for this are rare and trivial, there may be no need to worry. But watch that you're not waving your excuses in the face of red flags.

There were many red flags in Victor and Carol's relationship. Unfortunately, she chose not to see them. If you have to make excuses for someone or rationalize his behavior to make the relationship work . . . it's wrong; move on.

LOVE REJOICES
IN THE TRUTH
Lesson Three

If you have to make excuses for your partner or rationalize his behavior to make the relationship work . . . move on.

Wedding **Bells** OR WARNING **Bells?**

- He's elusive.

- He is chronically late for family gatherings, especially when it's your family.

- He lies.

- He blames everyone else for his problems.

- He never forgives and he never forgets.

- He is too dependent on you.

- He never says "I'm sorry."

- He constantly talks about his ex-girlfriend.

- He's demanding of everyone . . . except himself.

WHY MARRIAGE?

Marriage, with its sustaining rituals developed over centuries, can offer a refuge from the cares of the world, a place where you can take shelter with your beloved. Many studies show that married people live longer, healthier lives, and even have fewer problems with substance abuse and depression. Sure, there are all those old jokes: *Do married people live longer? No! It just feels like it; Marriage is not a word. It's a sentence—a life sentence;* and *A marriage certificate is just another word for a work permit.* I guess they should be expected. They should also be ignored.

A wedding offers two people the opportunity to declare their love for each other. Marriage offers the chance to live out that love together. Decision and declaration are what's important here, as is intention. Sure, in some cases marriage may be the result of momentum, the last act of the dating game. For the most part, however, the decision to get married is an informed one, guided by intention and not infatuation. Most couples take seriously the decision to get married—to make a declaration not of independence, but of *inter*dependence—and they take seriously the significance of their vows.

Consider these loving declarations:

- *I am standing before family and friends to take your hand as my partner.*
- *I take you to be my wife, to have and to hold, from this day forward, for better or for worse, for richer, for poorer, in sickness and in health, to love and to cherish, until death do us part.*
- *I take you to be my loving and lawfully wedded husband, my constant friend, my faithful partner, and my love from this day forward.*
- *In the presence of God, our family, and friends, I offer you my solemn vow to be your faithful partner in sickness and in health, in good times and in bad, and in joy as well as in sorrow.*
- *I promise to love you unconditionally, to support you in your goals, to honor and respect you, to laugh with you and cry with you, and to cherish you for as long as we both shall live.*

⊰ *I pledge to cherish our union and love you*
more each day than I did the day before.

Look at the words these couples use: *love, cherish, constant friend, faithful partner.* Good things, indeed, and they come with a promise, a pledge, or an offering. Talk about intention!

So, take your marriage vows seriously and know that should richer turn to poorer or health to sickness, only by performing the daily acts that, in their accumulation, uphold the marriage vows, will both individuals within the union be nourished.

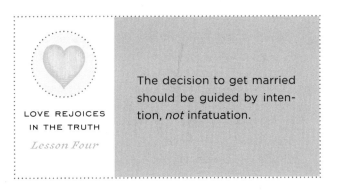

LOVE REJOICES
IN THE TRUTH

Lesson Four

The decision to get married should be guided by intention, *not* infatuation.

Dear Father Pat

Dear Father Pat: My boyfriend and I moved in with each other a few months ago and I'm concerned that he doesn't do his fair share of the chores unless I get annoyed with him, which I don't like doing. I love him very much, but his laziness is getting on my nerves and it's causing me to rethink the whole thing. Signed: *Lend a Hand*

Dear Lend a Hand: You're learning what men and women the world over have learned, that dating is one thing, cohabitating is quite another. I'm betting that you and your boy-friend moved in together without giving it enough thought as to what you both want from the relationship. Take the opportunity now to discuss your issues with him with-out getting annoyed. If you can't come to an agreement—and if he can't act on that agree-ment—then it's time to ask for his assistance on one last chore, helping you to move out.

The majority of couples who come to me to prepare for marriage are living together, even though most of them are Catholics, whose church frowns on the practice—to say the least.

In 1960 less than half a million couples lived together before marriage. In 1998 the Census Bureau reported that number to be over four million. There are many reasons for this dramatic increase. For one thing, even though family members may disapprove of the custom, it is tolerated these days and rarely spoken of as "living in sin." For another, couples are getting married at a much later age, often in their early thirties. Is it fair, the question is asked, to require such couples to refrain from sexual activity for so long and during that time in their lives when their sex drive is most powerful? Also, the fact that the divorce rate is so high makes couples leery of getting married. Better to try it out first, the argument goes, before taking the plunge.

*I wouldn't dream of marrying someone
I hadn't lived with. That's like
buying shoes you haven't tried on.*

—DR. JOYCE BROTHERS

Dr. Joyce Brothers, that pre-Dr. Phil, pre-Oprah expert on the art of relationships, is in favor of couples cohabiting before marriage. For Dr. Brothers, common sense and common law go together. But the consensus of studies made about living together seems to disagree with her. Some studies show that those who live together are more likely to divorce later on in their marriage—indeed 50 percent more likely. Other studies show that the divorce rate is higher for couples who live together for more than three years. Moreover, those who have cohabited may show evidence of not finding married life as satisfying as they had expected.

I can't tell you what to do.

Whether or not you decide to live together before

marriage is your decision. That said, never let your boyfriend pressure you into moving in together. If this is a route you're considering, you both must choose it freely and together. But know what you're getting into and what you want.

I suggest that you have a discussion with your partner about what "stage" moving in together constitutes in your relationship. Is it a precursor to marriage, a way to allay fears and, as Dr. Brothers would say, "to try each other on?" Or is it something just for now, a way to save on rent and consolidate your furniture? Having this discussion before you move in together might very well influence your decision.

LOVE REJOICES
IN THE TRUTH

Lesson Five

Don't let anyone pressure you into living together before marriage. Know what you're getting into and what you want.

Some cohabiting couples, precisely because they don't have a committed relationship that encompasses both present *and* future—or, dare I say, for better or worse—are reluctant to bring up big picture questions for fear of frightening the other partner away. But if it's risky to bring important matters out into the open, think how risky it is to tamp them down. Many cohabiting couples tend not to talk about the important issues that married couples have to face—children, finances, goals in life, jobs. Are you prepared to leave such things to chance?

ON THE MONEY

Men and women who live together outside of marriage are usually independent in their use of money. This is hardly a preparation for marriage, where interdependence is the name of the game. Things like saving for a house or longer-term expenditures may not come up when a couple is living together. If one party falls sick when a couple is cohabiting, the healthy partner has no responsibilities to pay for the other's medical expenses. It's different in marriage.

Questions for Couples Who Are Thinking of Living Together

Are you living together *prior* to marriage—or *instead* of it?

Is your decision to live together motivated more by fear (of potential divorce, of financial pressures, of loneliness) than by love?

Do you feel that your knowledge of one another will deepen?

Will living together strengthen your commitment to one another?

Have you expressed plainly to one another the cause of your reluctance to marry? Can you put to rest your worries?

What is the source of your newfound strength and resolve?

Do your family and friends support your decision?

The reality is that couples not committed in marriage are more likely to walk away from a relationship under challenging circumstances or when the going gets tough. And this often happens when money is involved.

After you marry, every asset either of you acquires is jointly held. That's why you both need to be in sync on your long-term financial goals, from paying off the mortgage to putting away for retirement. Ideally, you should talk about all this before you wed. If you don't, you can end up deeply frustrated and financially spent.

—SUZE ORMAN

THE BUSINESS OF MARRIAGE

Some people like to compartmentalize their lives. As one young man told me, "I think that marriage is like a small business, with each partner having his or her own jobs to do."

His fiancée seemed unsure. "I want to share our life," she said, "not approach it as though we are checking off a list of responsibilities. Am I missing something in his comparison of marriage to a small business?"

> *Marriage is not just a spiritual communion, it is also remembering to take out the trash.*
>
> —DR. JOYCE BROTHERS

I can understand why the concept of marriage as a small business is appealing to this young man. He needs to contain his anxieties about his approaching wedding, so, a small-business owner himself, he wants to use the familiar to come to terms with the big unknown that is marriage. That makes sense. Certainly, as comparisons go, I've heard worse. The way this young fiancé is thinking shows an understanding that marriage is more than the next stage in love and infatuation. Married life is as much about responsibility as it is about romance, and this young man seems to get that. Still, I'd caution him to put on the brakes before drafting the job descriptions for Mr. and Mrs.

The analogy of marriage to a small business is incomplete because it addresses only one part of married life, namely the sharing of responsibilities. But what about immeasurable concepts like intimacy? Business partners don't need to be intimate with one another—married couples must. The two of you need to sit down and take an inventory (now there's a good business word!) of your expectations, and talk frankly about all that goes into married life, like children, sex, forgiveness, in-laws. There's more to marriage than a business sense.

LOVE REJOICES
IN THE TRUTH

Lesson Six

Don't neglect talking about those immeasurable concepts like intimacy.

YOUR MARRIAGE INVENTORY

Fill in your thoughts on each of the following:

My partner's most admirable quality is...................

....

....

My partner's least admirable quality is..................

....

....

I feel most comfortable with my future partner when

....

....

....

I feel most uncomfortable with my future partner

when ....

....

....

I see the promise of marriage as ....

....

....

What worries me most about marriage ....

....

....

Sex is ....

....

....

When it comes to sexual pleasure our needs are ......

....

....

Sex without tenderness is ....

....

....

My parents' child-rearing methods were ....

....

....

We will raise our children ....

....

....

Talk about: I wish to live with you till death do us

part...

....

....

Talk about: fidelity ....

....

....

YOUR BODY, YOUR GIFT

Is there a strong physical attraction to the other? There used to be, in one of the formulas used at weddings, a wonderful sentence that was said by each spouse in turn: "With my body, I thee worship." It was presumed that each spouse would revel in making love to the other, each one making a gift of his/her body to the other unreservedly, worshipfully. If you feel no physical attraction to the other, don't marry him! If you need to make it work, it might be wise to see a sex therapist.

Don't marry a man to whom you feel no physical attraction.

I recently watched the movie *License to Wed*, a hilarious parody of the marriage preparation program that you would have to complete if you were to marry a Catholic. That movie was an interesting, if over-the-top, look at how this course works.

In one scene, the priest, played by Robin Williams, makes an unannounced visit to the apartment of an engaged couple to discuss their sex life, and proceeds to ask them some intimate questions:

Father Frank: Talking about sex, does it make you uncomfortable, Ben?

Ben: No, having you in my living room, talking about sex—that makes me uncomfortable.

Here are some questions that are essential for the
bride and groom to answer completely and honestly.
I know that these could be asked separately, with the
bride and groom in different rooms, but the sexual
side of marriage is the most intimate, so why make
them separate now?

- *Has your love grown since you became serious about one another?*
- *Do you see in this person the qualities you want in your children?*
- *Do you love each other with equal intensity and are you sure your love is not one-sided?*
- *Do you have a sense of confidence and trust in your partner?*
- *Do you know whether he will be a source of strength for whatever difficulties may come during your married life?*
- *Do you think that good fortune or bad will happen to you as a couple—and will you be able to accept it as such?*
- *Is there a strong physical attraction to your loved one?*

**LOVE REJOICES
IN THE TRUTH**

Lesson Seven

A mutual physical attraction is necessary for a happy marriage.

....

The Seven Lessons of
Love Does Not Rejoice in Wrongdoing, But Rejoices in the Truth

1. To achieve peace in your marriage, you must do things that *lead* to peace.

2. Insight is a valuable commodity for daily life and a necessity for marriage.

3. If you have to make excuses for your partner or rationalize his behavior to make the relationship work . . . move on.

4. The decision to get married should be guided by intention, *not* infatuation.

5. Don't let anyone pressure you into living together before marriage. Know what you're getting into and what you want.

6. Don't neglect talking about those immeasurable concepts like intimacy.

7. A mutual physical attraction is necessary for a happy marriage.

....

EIGHT

. . . .

Love Bears All Things, Believes All Things, Hopes All Things, Endures All Things. Love Never Gives Up.

Look Back in Laughter

A couple at whose wedding I officiated some ten years ago tells me that each year, on the anniversary of their wedding day, after banishing their two children to the TV room, they sit down at their kitchen table with the video of their wedding, including my sermon, an exercise fraught with unproductive nostalgia. When they have stopped laughing and crying, they each write down what they think of one another after so many years of married life—a hazardous experience, but one in which growth and maturity can occur.

JOHANNA'S STORY

Johanna had come to me some weeks before her tenth wedding anniversary. She and her husband were renewing their vows and wanted me to perform the ceremony. "It would be an honor," I told her.

As we sat down to talk about her plans for the anniversary celebration, she told me about something that happened when she was a nervous bride-to-be. "When I was planning my wedding I broke an antique lead crystal wineglass that my husband and I intended to use for the toast," Johanna told me. The wineglass, which had been in her family for years, was part of a set. One glass had the words *Forever Love* etched on it, while the other, the one with the broken stem, said *Forever True*. Johanna tried not to be superstitious, but in her pre-wedding jitters she worried it might be a sign.

Johanna burst into tears as she told her mother about the broken glass. "Mom tried to calm me down. She told me that it wasn't important, that it was just a glass after all. But I couldn't help it. It seemed that all my fears about getting married had found their object in that broken glass."

Johanna's mother went online to find someone who could repair the glass. It wasn't easy, but in the end she found a place about an hour's drive from their house.

"The shop was run by a lovely older couple," Johanna continued. "A husband and wife who were probably in their seventies at the time."

Apparently Mr. and Mrs. Gemmell had worked together for many years—she tending to customers at the front of the store, he taking care of the repairs in the back. From the description that Johanna gave me, it seemed that this shop had been bustling in its day, but no longer. It was quiet now. "One of those sweet relics of the past that will soon be gone" was how Johanna put it.

Being eighty myself, I didn't have much difficulty picturing this *relic*.

"I know I was only twenty-three," Johanna said, "but there was something about this place that made me feel wistful. Maybe it was the way Mrs. Gemmell brought me a cup of tea while I waited for her husband to repair the glass. Maybe it was the way she kept calling me 'dear.' Who knows? But she sat me down and listened with great care as I told her the details of my wedding. I had the feeling that she was recalling her own march down the aisle, many years ago. And as she was looking back I couldn't help but look forward. Would my husband and I make such partners as these two had?

> *I am a good friend to my husband.*
> *I have tried to make my marriage*
> *vows mean what they say. I show*
> *up. I listen. I try to laugh.*
>
> —ANNA QUINDLEN

"This woman was very sweet, and she was perceptive too," Johanna told me. "She took my hand and said, 'Tell me, dear—what's bothering you?'

"I tried to tell her that everything was all right, that I was just busy with the wedding, but she wasn't buying it.

" 'These old eyes might not see as well as they did, but I know when something's wrong.' Well, that's all it took," Johanna said. "I burst into tears . . . and then I told her the whole story. What there was of it, anyway."

Johanna was smiling at the memory.

"Mrs. Gemmell looked at me with such kindness, I felt a little relieved. And then I asked the question that had plagued me since the glass broke: 'Do you think it's a bad sign? You know. Broken glass . . . broken marriage?'

" 'It's a sign that the glass is old,' she said with a smile. 'That's all there is to it. Think of all the broken glasses in the world. Now think of all the happy marriages. There is absolutely no connection between the two, I assure you. Don't you spend any time worrying about this, my dear. Your love is strong, it's not fragile like glass. I can tell. Besides, things break in every relationship—it's how you put them back together

**LOVE ENDURES
ALL THINGS**

Lesson One

Things go wrong in every relationship. It's how you address the wrong that counts.

that matters. You go off and have a wonderful wedding . . . and a wonderful life.'

"You know, Father Pat—every year my husband and I use those glasses to toast our anniversary. We give our first toast to each other. We give the second to Mrs. Gemmell."

THE TRUTH ABOUT TRUE LOVE

"I am dating a man who says he does not believe that true love exists," one young woman confided. "Why would he say that?"

"Ask him," I said.

She smiled at the simplicity of my answer.

"Really," I said again. "Ask him. Find out how he defines *true love*. Better yet, ask him how he defines both *true* and *love* separately, then ask him if he has experienced any sort of love in his life."

"I'm not sure I understand," she said. "Doesn't everyone know what *true love* means?"

"But no! And now you have an opportunity to open up a discussion that not enough people enter into. So often we take for granted our notions of what true love is. We conjure up experiences from our own lives—real or imagined. We bring in impressions from books and movies and from the relationships around us. From these experiences we base not just our idea of love, but our *ideal* of love."

Love is an ideal thing,
marriage a real thing.

—GOETHE

She nodded. Poor girl. She should have realized that would only encourage me to continue.

"There's every chance that your friend is having something of an allergic reaction to the hearts and flowers industry," I said. "You know, that great machine that pumps out Valentine's Day cards, scented candles, romantic comedies, and those ridiculously sweet stuffed toys that say things like *I wuve you.*

"Or perhaps he's bristling against the notion of a *soul mate*, the idea that there's one person and one alone who will *complete you* or serve as your *better half.* If that's the case I think you've got a sensible young man there. I too disagree with the concept of the soul mate, with the idea that there is some soul predestined by heaven to be your one and only match. It's an idea that seems to imply that when you find The One you will fit seamlessly together, like two pieces of a puzzle, without intention or effort on your part. What pressure! What poppycock!"

My young friend just smiled.

"Now," I continued, "he may not say that he believes in true love. But does he nevertheless say 'I love you' to you? If so, what does he mean by that? Does his behavior toward you, despite his protestations,

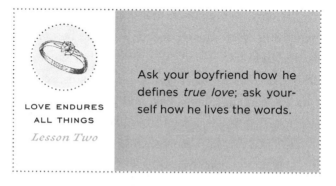

LOVE ENDURES ALL THINGS

Lesson Two

Ask your boyfriend how he defines *true love*; ask yourself how he lives the words.

meet *your* definition of love? He may just be putting on this mask of cynicism as the only way to cope with a tough world out there. Listen to what he says, and watch what he does. And if you're contemplating marriage to this young man, be sure that you enter into a respectful and meaningful conversation about your relationship *before* you make the commitment."

What Is Love?

Love is a choice you make from moment to moment.—Barbara de Angelis

Love is an emotion experienced by the many and enjoyed by the few.—George Jean Nathan

Love is a promise, love is a souvenir, once given never forgotten, never let it disappear.—John Lennon

Love is the only force capable of transforming an enemy into friend.—Martin Luther King, Jr.

Love is a condition in which the happiness of another person is essential to your own.—Robert Heinlein

DON'T BE AFRAID

You may feel you can never live up to the standards of marriage that you have set for yourself. As your wedding approaches you may find yourself staggering beneath this sense of impossibility. Fear is a normal part of life. Even the Bible acknowledges that. Did you know that the simple and beautiful phrase "Don't be afraid" appears 365 times throughout that book? That's once for every day of the year. Use this as a mantra whenever fear rears its ugly head.

But that's easy for me to say. I've found myself standing on the altar a great many times, but I've never had to walk down the aisle to meet my intended. What a frightening prospect that must be! I guess that's why sometimes, as her wedding day approaches, a bride-to-be will suffer a meltdown. I would never use the term *Bridezilla*, but I must say that I've seen some pretty wild performances. In most cases, I've found that the bride's behavior is provoked by the fear that she will let down her partner, that she won't be a good wife.

Everybody has issues. And everybody has fears. Many husbands-to-be are also feeling the same way, and acting out the same way too. It's a shame that

> *When you make a sacrifice in marriage, you're sacrificing not to each other but to unity in a relationship.*
>
> —JOSEPH CAMPBELL

nobody's coined the term *Groomzilla!* So first step, acknowledge that this premarital fear is normal for the both of you. You're about to make a life-altering promise to one another. That's enough to make *anyone* nervous. However, if you are fearful that you won't live up to your partner's expectations, tell him about it. Talk to him in a thoughtful way, using specific examples.

- *What about yourself—or about him—are you afraid of?*
- *What is it about your forthcoming marriage that you fear the most?*

That could lead to a fruitful, groundbreaking conversation.

If you've had a year's engagement, if you've had counseling and have asked each other the appropriate *Why are we getting married?* questions, then you have every chance of the *happily ever after* that you both desire. Take a deep breath and remind yourself: "You have nothing to fear but fear itself." And perhaps the caterer.

That said, while pre-wedding fears are perfectly normal and usually baseless, it's important to distinguish between pre-wedding jitters and a real solid fear about your partner. Pre-wedding-day jitters are normal. However, if leading up to your wedding day you feel a nameless anxiety about marrying this man, hold off until you've allayed those fears. If you can't allay them, don't marry him!

**LOVE ENDURES
ALL THINGS**

Lesson Three

If you can't allay serious pre-wedding-day fears, don't marry him.

MR. RIGHT OR MR. RIGHT OVER THERE?

I've heard it many times. Women will be engaged and deeply in love, yet still feel attracted to other men.

"I am engaged," one woman told me. "I'd never do anything to hurt my relationship, yet sometimes I feel attracted to other men. I even develop a little crush on them." At this point she twisted her engagement ring around her finger. "I would never act on these impulses, but why does this happen? I know no one will ever fit me like my fiancé does, and no one could ever replace him. Does my ego just need boosting?"

You say: "No one will ever fit me as my fiancé does," and "No one could ever replace him." These statements are not quite true.

You feel as confused as you do because there is not just one person who is the only one you could be successfully engaged to.

There are many Mr. Rights. A lasting marriage is based on many things: love, shared goals, a desire to carve out a life together. But meeting that person that you are going to decide will be that Mr. Right has more to do with chance than destiny. As you go through life, you will meet numerous men you could be successfully married to. When you have made your choice, rejoice in that, commit to that, and do what you can to make it work.

LOVE ENDURES ALL THINGS

Lesson Four

There are many possible Mr. Rights. When you've chosen the man who is to be yours, rejoice in that decision and commit to it.

ONE PERFECT DAY

"Once I accepted the proposal," one engaged woman said, "I started worrying about the wedding."

"We had no money," the groom explained. "Our parents had no money."

"I am perversely pleased," I said, "that you have no money to pay for your wedding. This means that on your wedding day you will be focusing on essentials like your vows, or the readings, and not on nonessentials, like the color of the bridesmaids' dresses. You'll be starting your married life off on the right foot. And no priest or minister will refuse to officiate at your wedding because you are broke!"

So take heart.

When a tornado devastated the community of McGee, Mississippi, on a Thursday in March 2009, one couple was anticipating their wedding the upcoming Saturday. The local church, where the wedding was to take place, was destroyed. As the bride stood vigil on the outskirts of the ruins of the church, the minister promised the bride that her wedding would still go on as planned, that together they would find a location for her guests to gather. In spite of the calamitous overtones brought forth by the natural disaster, here was an occasion where the purity of the event was celebrated in its spiritual essence.

Time and again I have heard people who were penniless in their early married life say that the situation brought them closer together as they lovingly supported one another during times of genuine hardship.

I try to dissuade couples from the belief that

seems to be held increasingly in common: that establishment of great financial worth must necessarily precede an engagement. Here again, many people seem to confuse the wedding with the marriage. You can be forgiven in that. There's a lot of pressure on soon-to-be-marrieds to design the perfect fairy-tale wedding.

By 2006, according to the calculations of Condé Nast, the American wedding industry was worth $161 billion to the United States economy, with the average expenditure on a single wedding averaging $28,000.

It need not be thus. Take notice of the marriage ritual, within which is contained the mystery of commitment. It is a public ritual, celebrated before all those who will function as the couple's personal community thereafter. The rich tradition, the exchange of vows and rings, and the blessing and the prayers over the new marriage, all culminate in that ultimate dedication by the couple of their lives to one another.

**LOVE ENDURES
ALL THINGS**

Lesson Five

Don't confuse the wedding
with the marriage.

SPEAKING OF LOVE

"Would you be willing to enter a lifelong conversation with me?" asked one man of his intended bride.

Contrast this with the English novelist Evelyn Waugh's proposal to his first wife: "Why don't we try marriage and see how it goes?" Hardly the best start to a life together.

We've all heard stories of fun or quirky proposals. The guy who chooses the scoreboard at the football game to ask for his girlfriend's hand. The couple who elopes to Vegas on a whim. Think about it. The decision to get married will affect your entire life. Do you really want to enter into something so casually?

A relationship that's governed by respect should be matched by a respectful proposal. A loving, thoughtful proposal sets the tone for the emotional tenor of the marriage.

One couple I talked to shared this story of the moment they became engaged.

"For me the event is tinted with nostalgia, like one of those *Prairie Home Companion* episodes," began the groom. "I remember the emotion of the moment, but I don't remember a lot of details. It was beautiful out. She was upset at that time that I was going to be traveling in Russia for several months."

"I was sure he was going to meet Katerina or Svetlana . . . ," she said.

I heard possible overtones of jealousy in her words, and, knowing what a detriment jealousy can be in married life, wondered if the narrative was about to take an unexpected turn.

"It was already twelve thirty, one o'clock in the morning," the groom continued. "The moon was full. We'd had a barbecue. We were sitting on the skate ramp and she was crying. And I asked," he said, " 'what would it take to convince you that I feel every bit as much for you as you do for me?'

LOVE ENDURES
ALL THINGS

Lesson Six

A loving, thoughtful proposal sets the tone for the emotional tenor of the marriage.

"So I said," he continued, " 'I would like to propose marriage to you right now. I would like you to be my fiancée, right here under the light of the moon. I have nothing to give you except my word, but I would like you to think about this.' I proposed to her on a skate ramp in my backyard."

I was pleased to hear the groom's remark, "I would like you to think about this." It's a good sign to see a man not rushing his wife-to-be into the decision to commit.

The couple showed me their rings. "We bought these rings," the groom said, "one for fifteen dollars, one for twenty. We plan someday to upgrade to sterling silver or surgical steel. Maybe platinum."

I'm glad, I told them, that you didn't spend too much on the rings. I hope you forget in the future getting more expensive rings, of silver or platinum. Put the money toward your children's college funds!

 Wedding **Bells** WARNING **Bells?**

⊲ E-mail! He proposed via e-mail!!! I was so outraged I sent it to my spam filter.—Barbara J.

⊲ He popped the question while we were waiting on line at McDonald's.—Linette V.

⊲ Unbelievable, but he got his best friend to ask me. I turned them both down.—Mary L.

⊲ He texted me and didn't even include a smiley. —Katherine N.

⊲ It was April 13th and he was doing his taxes. He asked me if maybe we could file jointly next year.—Miriam F.

LOVE IS AGELESS

A young woman once asked me if age is a factor in determining whether you are ready to be married. "I have a friend," she said, "who is nineteen and engaged, yet I know other people who wait to wed until they are in their thirties or even forties."

"I have known young people who are remarkably mature in their outlook and their actions," I told her. "And I have known middle-aged people who refuse to grow up. So, as always, generalizations are dangerous."

When I was a teenager a teenage friend of mine fell in love with a fifteen-year-old girl. Neither of them looked at anyone else, and, of course, they came in for a lot of teasing from us insensitive types. As soon as they could, they married, and are still going strong, fifty years later.

The trick, when you are looking for a partner, is to remember that the ones (I use the plural deliberately) who manifest my signs of maturity will be good risks for marriage. I also use the word *risk* deliberately, because you can pick out the most mature person in the neighborhood for your spouse and things can still go wrong. Marriage is a calculated risk, but enter into it with your eyes open and you'll lessen the risk tremendously.

With people living longer these days I have officiated at a number of weddings where the bride and groom are older than I am. Long live romance! Such couples don't agree with my revered Samuel Johnson, who once said: "Second marriages are the triumph of hope over experience!" In a given year nearly half of all marriages are remarriages for one or both partners.

An older woman was sitting on a park bench on a spring day. A gentleman of similar age seated himself next to her.

Looking over at him, she remarked, "You look just like my third husband."

"Really," the gentleman replied. "How many times have you been married?"

She looked at him and smiled. "Twice."

FORGIVE AND FORGET

A forgiving spirit is a necessity for married life.

Some hints on the art of forgiving:

Never forget that the person who has hurt you is a human being worthy of being treated with dignity, even when he has hurt you. Remember that he is a child of God, made in the image and likeness of God. The possession of these dignities demands that he be forgiven. Another way of putting it is to separate what the person has done to you from who he is.

> *We are told that people stay in love because of chemistry, or because they remain intrigued with each other, because of many kindnesses, because of luck. But part of it has got to be forgiveness and gratefulness.*
>
> —ELLEN GOODMAN

Forgiving is not the same as forgetting.

Forgetting often takes time.

I like to tell the story of Clara Barton, founder of the American Red Cross. A friend asked her if she remembered a terrible hurt done to her some time in the past. "No," said Clara, "I distinctly remember forgetting it."

Saint Augustine gave us two aphorisms on forgiveness. Said he: "Never believe that your enemy can do you more harm than your own enmity." Beautiful.

Translation: Our unforgiving spirit hurts us more than the person who did the deed ever did.

I remember years ago a fellow priest brutally destroyed a community of the faithful I had helped to build up. I was outraged! I would lie awake at night, thinking of how I would treat him when I saw him again. Would I snub him? Would I run him through with the harpoon of my wit? Would I give him the cold shoulder? There I was, eaten up by the desire for some form of retaliation, while presumably he was in a deep sleep, blissfully unaware that I was tossing and turning, dreaming up methods of revenge.

Yet, there is Augustine's second principle of forgiveness, "Never [like most reformed sinners, he liked to begin sentences with *Never*] believe that the hurt someone inflicts on you arose entirely outside yourself." Translation, for me, anyhow: When someone hurts me, I more often than not have to admit that I am partly the cause of this person's behavior toward me. I provoked him with my own insensitivity or arrogance, or unwillingness to listen.

What else might make forgiveness a little bit easier to practice?

A family therapist friend of mine reminds me that some people deal with their own pain by dealing out pain to others. Have you noticed that about yourself? You've been hurt, and the only way you can deal with your pain is by lashing out at the other, who is flabbergasted by your incomprehensible behavior.

Years ago, I was chaplain at a large city hospital. The recently appointed head nurse in one of the wards was detested by the other nurses under her. Then, one of the nurses discovered that before the

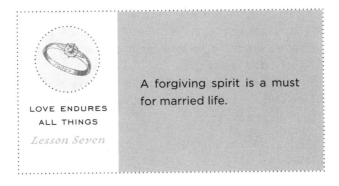

LOVE ENDURES
ALL THINGS
Lesson Seven

A forgiving spirit is a must for married life.

head nurse had taken up her position, her five-year-old son had drowned in a backyard pool. The nurses' attitude toward their superior changed from one of hostility and resentment to one of understanding and compassion, with the result that soon the head nurse responded in kind.

Love Is a Long-Distance Runner

Years ago I used to do some work in a local prison. The authorities brought down to this prison a young man from North Jersey to serve his sentence. Every first Sunday was "visiting Sunday," so his father would make the drive to the prison—more than two hours each way—to visit his son. Every month, his son refused to see him. Every month, down the father came again. One Sunday I took the opportunity to ask the father why he persisted in his visits when his son refused to see him.

"I want him to know how much I love him," he said. "I can't think of any other way to do it."

Love never gives up.

....

The Seven Lessons of
*Love Bears All Things,
Believes All Things, Hopes All
Things, Endures All Things.
Love Never Gives Up.*

1. Things go wrong in every relationship. It's how you address the wrong that counts.

2. Ask your boyfriend how he defines *true love*; ask yourself how he lives the words.

3. If you can't allay serious pre-wedding-day fears, don't marry him.

4. There are many possible Mr. Rights. When you've chosen the man who is to be yours, rejoice in that decision and commit to it.

5. Don't confuse the wedding with the marriage.

6. A loving, thoughtful proposal sets the tone for the emotional tenor of the marriage.

7. A forgiving spirit is a must for married life.

....

Ask Father Pat

I want two or three children but my boyfriend doesn't really like kids. I figure that once we're married I can work on him to change his mind. My sister says this is a really bad idea.

Your sister is right. People are the same after the wedding day as they are before—sometimes even more so. Work on him to change his socks. Work on him to change his underwear. But don't work on him to change his mind. It's not going to happen.

I found out that my fiancé spent the night with his ex-girlfriend. He told me that he was scared and that he just went back to her to make sure he made the right decision. He was really upset and asked me to forgive him. I love Josh, but how can I forgive him if I don't know whether I can trust him?

It's quite possible that he's made a one-time mistake, but it's a pretty big one. Again, this is why I advise a longer engagement period, so that your husband-to-be can really show that he is capable of fidelity. If he's afraid, he should be talking to you, his girlfriend, not his ex-girlfriend. It's one thing to have cold feet. It's quite another to get them warmed by another woman. My advice? Don't marry him.

. . . .

Do you believe in love at first sight?

Yes, because I've seen it firsthand! My mother, Patricia, when asked what attracted her to my father, Herbert Eli Connor, replied: "I liked the shape of his neck." Now if that isn't love at first sight, I don't know what is! But let's not get carried away. Love at first sight may not prove to be a reliable guide to a committed relationship. So if you find yourself smitten, give love time to prove itself. And remember, there are other ingredients to a successful marriage.

. . . .

I'm a Christian and my boyfriend is a Muslim. We know that we face hurdles in our relationship, but are committed to working things through. The problem is our parents, who are dead set against the match. Any advice?

Communication is the name of the game here. So as soon as you think you're getting serious, talk to each other's families. The odds are your parents know little about the Muslim faith, so a respectful face-to-face will be helpful to everyone. Make sure your boyfriend knows beforehand that your parents are concerned about your relationship and will expect some frank answers from him. And be prepared to meet his family on the same terms.

If your parents are adamant in rejecting him, and you still want to marry him, you may have to bite the bullet and do so despite their objections. It wouldn't be the first time that a woman (or a man) has married against parents' wishes. It's unlikely to be the last.

. . . .

My boyfriend wants me to sign a pre-nup. I'm insulted. Not only does it show a lack of trust on his part, but I think it's a bad idea to go into a marriage with thoughts that it won't work out. Who's right?

In this day and age, when 50 percent of marriages end up in divorce, I can see how a couple (after exhaustively talking about the issue) could sign a pre-nup. Marriage is a daunting prospect, and money problems are the source of many failed marriages. Could this be a sign that you and your fiancé don't see eye-to-eye on financial matters? This crucial area of married life deserves a lot of discussion. Still, if you and your fiancé can't come to agreement, I would give the same advice that any good lawyer would—don't sign anything you're not comfortable with.

. . . .

My boyfriend has a child from his previous marriage. Danny loves his daughter and sees her every Saturday. He's a really good dad. Last week when we were picking up Alisha, his ex made some kind of nasty comment about Danny being late with his child support payments. It got me thinking. If Danny isn't doing the right thing for his little girl, can he really be the stand-up guy I thought he was?

Ask him. There can be any number of reasons why he's late with the payments, if in fact he is. This is another example of my basic rule of communication: "Speak the truth to one another in love." Don't accuse him. You love him, so find out what his story is, and *then* make the judgment.

My mother really likes my boyfriend. She says he's "marriage material" and that I should snap him up before someone else does. I'm not so sure.

Tell your mother to marry him! **In all seriousness, it's lovely to have your mother's approval, but it is you who has to see him as "marriage material."**

I've recently found out that my fiancé has a drug problem. I love him deeply, but I don't want to be married to an addict.

Do not, under any circumstances, marry him with just the promise that he'll get straight. A sustained long-term commitment to living drug-free is what's important here. Your fiancé's getting clean (and living clean) must be a condition of marriage. This, by the way, is why I don't believe in the notion of unconditional love. There are times when you have to impose conditions on your loved one. This is one of them.

....

My boyfriend and I have a strong relationship. We love each other deeply and want to get married. The only problem is our families don't get along. Should I be worried?

First, ask why they don't get along, because your families may see something that you've missed. Communication is key here, with your family and also with your fiancé. How does he deal with this mutual estrangement? It may tell you something about him you didn't know, because we are largely what our families make us. Still, it remains to be said, your relationship with the family of your spouse-to-be does not determine your relationship with your spouse. If you've thought this through carefully, I suggest getting married anyway. Just make sure to keep the lines of communication open on all fronts.

....